REGENTS RENAISSANCE DRAMA SERIES

General Editor: Cyrus Hoy
Advisory Editor: G. E. Bentley

EPICOENE

BEN JONSON

Epicoene
or
The Silent Woman

Edited by

L. A. BEAURLINE

LONDON
EDWARD ARNOLD (PUBLISHERS) LTD.

Copyright © 1966 by the University of Nebraska Press
Published in Great Britain by Edward Arnold (Publishers) Ltd.
First Published in Great Britain 1967
Reprinted 1971

Cloth ISBN: 0 7131 5189 7
Paper ISBN: 0 7131 5190 0

Printed in Great Britain by
William Clowes and Sons Limited, London
Beccles and Colchester

Regents Renaissance Drama Series

The purpose of the Regents Renaissance Drama Series is to provide soundly edited texts, in modern spelling, of the more significant plays of the Elizabethan, Jacobean, and Caroline theater. Each text in the series is based on a fresh collation of all sixteenth- and seventeenth-century editions. The textual notes, which appear above the line at the bottom of each page, record all substantive departures from the edition used as the copy-text. Variant substantive readings among sixteenth- and seventeenth-century editions are listed there as well. In cases where two or more of the old editions present widely divergent readings, a list of substantive variants in editions through the seventeenth century is given in an appendix. Editions after 1700 are referred to in the textual notes only when an emendation originating in some one of them is received into the text. Variants of accidentals (spelling, punctuation, capitalization) are not recorded in the notes. Contracted forms of characters' names are silently expanded in speech prefixes and stage directions, and, in the case of speech prefixes, are regularized. Additions to the stage directions of the copy-text are enclosed in brackets. Stage directions such as "within" or "aside" are enclosed in parentheses when they occur in the copy-text.

Spelling has been modernized along consciously conservative lines. "Murther" has become "murder," and "burthen," "burden," but within the limits of a modernized text, and with the following exceptions, the linguistic quality of the original has been carefully preserved. The variety of contracted forms ('*em*, '*am*, '*m*, '*um*, '*hem*) used in the drama of the period for the pronoun *them* are here regularly given as '*em*, and the alternation between *a'th'* and *o'th'* (for *on* or *of the*) is regularly reproduced as *o'th'*. The copy-text distinction between preterite endings in -*d* and -*ed* is preserved except where the elision of *e* occurs in the penultimate syllable; in such cases, the final syllable is contracted. Thus, where the old editions read "threat'ned," those of the present series read "threaten'd." Where, in the old editions, a contracted preterite in -*y'd* would yield -*i'd* in modern spelling (as in "try'd," "cry'd," "deny'd"), the word is here given in its full form (e.g., "tried," "cried," "denied").

Punctuation has been brought into accord with modern practices. The effort here has been to achieve a balance between the generally light pointing of the old editions, and a system of punctuation which, without overloading the text with exclamation marks, semicolons, and dashes, will make the often loosely flowing verse (and prose) of the original syntactically intelligible to the modern reader. Dashes are regularly used only to indicate interrupted speeches, or shifts of address within a single speech.

Explanatory notes, chiefly concerned with glossing obsolete words and phrases, are printed below the textual notes at the bottom of each page. References to stage directions in the notes follow the admirable system of the Revels editions, whereby stage directions are keyed, decimally, to the line of the text before or after which they occur. Thus, a note on 0.2 has reference to the second line of the stage direction at the beginning of the scene in question. A note on 115.1 has reference to the first line of the stage direction following line 115 of the text of the relevant scene.

CYRUS HOY

University of Rochester

Contents

List of Abbreviations

Aubrey	John Aubrey. *Brief Lives*. Ed. A. Clark. Oxford, 1898.
Bald	*Epicoene*. Ed. R. C. Bald. In *Six Elizabethan Plays*. New York, 1963.
Camden	Carroll Camden. *The Elizabethan Woman*. New York, 1952.
conj.	conjecture
Cooper	Thomas Cooper. *Thesaurus Linguae Romanae & Britannicae*. London, 1578.
corr.	corrected; the second state of a press variant
correc.	correction
Cotgrave	Randle Cotgrave. *A Dictionarie of the French and English Tongues*. London, 1611.
Cunningham	*The Works of Ben Jonson*. Ed. William Gifford, with notes by Francis Cunningham. London, 1875.
F1	the first edition, in Jonson's folio, 1616
F1 (DFo6)	Jonson's folio, 1616, Folger copy 6, with manuscript notes
F2	the third edition, in Jonson's second folio, 1640
F3	the fourth edition, in Jonson's third folio, 1692
Gifford	*The Works of Ben Jonson*. Ed. William Gifford. London, 1816.
Henry	*Epicoene or The Silent Woman*. Ed. Aurelia Henry (Yale Studies in English, Vol. XXXI). New York, 1906.
H.S.	*Ben Jonson*. Ed. C. H. Herford, Percy and Evelyn Simpson. Oxford, 1925–1952.
MS1	Folger Library manuscript V.a.162
MS2	New York Public Library manuscript Drexel 4041
Nares	Robert Nares. *A Glossary*. Ed. J. O. Halliwell and Thomas Wright. London, 1882.
OED	*Oxford English Dictionary*
om.	omitted
orig.	the first setting of a forme

PMLA	*Publications of the Modern Language Association of America*
Q	the second edition, in quarto, 1620
reset	a reset forme, in entirely new type from the original
S.D.	stage direction
S.P.	speech prefix
STC	A. W. Pollard & G. R. Redgrave. *A Short-Title Catalogue of Books Printed in England . . . 1475–1640.* London, 1926.
Sugden	Edward H. Sugden. *A Typographical Dictionary of the Works of Shakespeare and his Fellow Dramatists.* Manchester, 1925.
Tilley	Morris Palmer Tilley. *A Dictionary of the Proverbs in England in the Sixteenth and Seventeenth Centuries.* Ann Arbor, 1950.
uncorr.	uncorrected; the first state of a press variant
Whalley	*The Workes of Ben Jonson.* Ed. Peter Whalley. London, 1756.

Introduction

THE PLAY

Dryden, who preferred it before all other plays, thought that the intrigue of *Epicoene* was "the greatest and most noble of any pure unmixed comedy in any language," and the whole play, he thought, was a pattern of correct writing, according to the French rules, but superior to the French, having more "variety of design" and more lively representation of human nature.[1] So it is not surprising that William Congreve, Dryden's protégé, imitated *Epicoene* in *The Way of the World*. Later critics, however, have had mixed reactions: Swinburne, who thought it an imperial farce, inferior to *Twelfth Night* although superior to *The Misanthrope*, was repelled by the "bull baiting and bear baiting brutality" that tinged it. Edmund Wilson found it "revolting in its forced barbarity," but significant because it reflected Jonson's unconscious anal eroticism. Recent critics, thinking Dryden misunderstood the play, have veered away from the discussion of its plot and sought to explain the unity or primal power in its imagery, its theme, or its prose style.

Dramatically speaking, what eventually draws *Epicoene* together is a spectacular stage device: casting the usual boy actor as a woman; marrying this unnatural silent woman to Morose; transforming her into the other extreme of monsterhood, a jabbering woman, a collegiate lady; sullying her reputation with tales of promiscuity; and finally, just when she has most fully created the illusion of an aggressive modern woman, a mannish creature, a very hermaphrodite—suddenly revealing that the illusion is the reality. Or more precisely, theatrical necessity is metamorphosed into dramatic life; the game is in earnest.

In the early seventeenth century, when verisimilitude had not yet fastened its restraints on the drama, Shakespeare also worked such an effect in *The Winter's Tale*; the actor playing Hermione had to play the statue of herself in order for the illusion of Act V, scene iii, to come

[1] John Dryden, *Of Dramatic Poesie*, ed. Ker. (1908), I, 83.

off, so the natural *coup de théâtre* was to bring the statue to life. Nothing
is more titillating in the theater than to build the stage illusion into
the plot, calling attention to the artifice at the same time that it is
transcended and drawn up into the illusion itself. Hence the popularity of the play within the play. You are carried along with the
pretense; your passions are moved "by such insinuating degrees
that you shall not choose but consent and go along with them" while
at the same time you "stand admiring the subtile tracks of your
engagement."[2] Of a Restoration performance Pepys remarked that

> it is an excellent play. Among other things here, Kinaston, the
> boy, had the good turn to appear in three shapes: first, as a poor
> woman in ordinary clothes, to please Morose; then in fine clothes,
> as a gallant, and in them was clearly the prettiest woman in the
> whole house, and lastly as a man; and then likewise did appear
> the handsomest man in the house.[3]

With the growth of the star system and a thoughtless assumption
that only a woman can credibly pretend to be a woman, leading
ladies such as Mrs. Knep, Mrs. Oldfield, Mrs. Pritchard, and the
indomitable Mrs. Siddons henceforth took the role. To make matters
worse, George Colman's adaptation of the script (1776) sentimen-
talized the play and softened the vexation. Garrick's company at
Drury Lane tried to revive it ("not acted these twenty years"), first
with a woman and then the second night with a boy in the title role.
Although the play was "received with particular approbation"
according to one review, it never recovered the popularity that it
enjoyed before 1750.[4] Gifford thought that *Epicoene* lost favor because
of these mistakes in casting, but between 1664 and 1750 it was solid
and reliable box office in spite of the actresses. The decline must have
been caused by something else. It was deemed "inappropriate to
contemporary intellect" and parts were "somewhat hissed" as
indecent. Possibly the visual pun offended the eighteenth century
because it was "false wit," and the whole play thought not to be
good-natured or amiable humor. With our recent interest in Piran-
dello and Giraudoux's theater of pretense and illusion, we would hope

[2] A paraphrase from James Shirley's preface to Beaumont and Fletcher's
Comedies and Tragedies (1647), sig. A3v.
[3] *Diary*, ed. Wheatley (1893), January 7, 1660/61.
[4] *The London Stage*, ed. Stone (1962), part 4, vol. III, p. 1946.

that some enterprising directors will restore *Epicoene* to its rightful place in the dramatic repertory.

Jonson did not invent the basic device of the play; he worked with a tradition of such disguises. Plautus, in his *Casina*, married a slave, disguised as a woman, to an old man, rival of his son. This was embellished in Ariosto's *Il Marescalco*, Jonson's immediate source, and in Machiavelli's *Clizia*, an analogue. Shakespeare's *Twelfth Night* may also have been in Jonson's mind. Earlier in the reign of James I, John Day's *The Isle of Gulls* (1606) was acted by the same company (then called the Children of Blackfriars) as *Epicoene*; in that play the new nobility, the king, the queen, their favorites, and the homosexuality of the English court were satirized through the use of a man disguised as a woman.[5] But in none of these plays did the playwright keep the secret from the audience; Jonson boldly violated one of the most elementary principles of the drama: never trick the audience. For the performance of *The Isle of Gulls*, some players were imprisoned, and for similar personal satire on the King the following year James closed their theater and "vowed they should never play more, but should first beg their bread."[6] But James liked plays almost as much as he liked bearbaiting and handsome young men; and by late 1609 or early 1610, the reformed Children's company opened in the renovated Whitefriars Theatre. One of their first plays was *Epicoene*.

Jonson wisely eschewed royal satire, but could not resist an allusion to a bounder, the Prince of Moldavia, Stephano Janiculo, who once escaped from a Turkish prison disguised as a woman and now pretended to be engaged to the King's cousin, Lady Arabella Stuart. Unfortunately, she had been recently confined by the wary King for promising her hand to an unnamed suitor (probably William Seymour, also of royal blood), and she complained "that in a certain comedy the playwright introduced an allusion to her person and the part played by the Prince of Moldavia. The play was suppressed."[7]

[5] John Day was apparently indebted not only to a well-known episode in Sidney's *Arcadia*, but also to *L'Isle des Hermaphrodites* (1605), a notorious satire on the court of Henry III of France, whom Jonson alludes to in *Epicoene*, IV.vi.27. Chapman's *Monsieur D'Olive* (1604) was another play in the same tradition.

[6] E. K. Chambers, *Elizabethan Stage* (Oxford, 1923), II, 54.

[7] Venetian Ambassador's letter, dated Feb. 8, 1609/10, *Calendar of State Papers Venetian* (1864), XI, no. 794, p. 427.

Jonson claimed, as he did too frequently to be convincing, that no personal slight was meant—"They made a libel, which he made a play"—but the lines in question are very ambiguous, concerning Sir John Daw's map-making (V.i.19–21):

CLERIMONT.

How, maps of persons!

LA FOOLE.

Yes, sir, of Nomentack, when he was here, and of the Prince of Moldavia, and of his mistress, Mistress Epicoene.

"His mistress" may mean Daw's mistress, but could easily be interpreted on the stage as Moldavia's mistress. Curiously, Lady Arabella played an epicene part two years later, when she escaped from confinement in the clothes of a boy.

Our difficulty in understanding this transvestism as did Jonson's contemporaries comes from our limited use of the terms "epicene" and "hermaphrodite." "Epicene" signified not just effeminacy, but a common gender, one grammatical form in Greek to indicate either sex. And the term "hermaphrodite" was not, in Jonson's time, used always in the strict biological sense. In the play it is obviously associated with all varieties of sexual metamorphosis. Women who sought independence of their husbands, who learned foreign tongues, who wore leather jerkins, or who painted with cosmetics were mannish women.[8] Men who wore feathers, played badminton, or submitted as "servants" to domineering mistresses were called womanish men, "very hermaphrodites." Two contemporary pamphlets attacked them under the titles *Hic Mulier; or, the man woman; being a medicine to cure the coltish disease of the staggers in the masculine-feminines of our times* (1620?, *STC* 13374) and *Haec-vir; or the womanish man: being an answere to the late booke intitled Hic mulier* (1620?, *STC* 12599).

Puritans attacked the hermaphroditical stage players for violation of scripture: "The woman shall not wear that which pertaineth unto a man, neither shall a man put on a woman's garment: for all that do so are abomination unto the Lord thy God" (*Deut.* 22:5), but almost any unnatural behavior might deserve the label. Jonson himself may have been taunting the Puritans with his boy as Epicoene, as he did in the puppet show of *Bartholomew Fair* (V.v.95–100), but the text makes much more of the excesses of fashionable ladies and

[8] Carroll Camden, *The Elizabethan Woman* (1952), pp. 263–267.

gentlemen. Jonson favored manly conduct for men and a manly, restrained style: "Clothes and titles are the birdlime of fools," the effeminate masks of ignorance and impudence (*Timber*, ed. H. S., VIII, 1435). Therefore we should recognize the analogy between Epicoene and the rest of the cast: in one way or another most of the satirized characters lose or distort their sexuality. The Collegiates live away from their husbands, pretend to learning, "cry down or up what they like or dislike in a brain or a fashion with most masculine or rather hermaphroditical authority," and they call each other by their last names as men do. La Foole is a "precious manikin," a "wind-fucker," who claims to have carnal knowledge of Epicoene, and suffers in Act IV a ritual castration. Daw, who also serves Epicoene, is a "mere talking mole! . . . a fellow so utterly nothing, as he knows not what he would be." Otter, an amphibian (i.e., of indeterminate sex) "is his wife's subject; he calls her princess." Mrs. Otter, Gorgon's head, an Amazon with a brazen throat, "takes herself asunder still when she goes to bed, into some twenty boxes, and about next day noon is put together again, like a great German clock." Epicoene herself, after her tongue loosens, is full of "Amazonian impudence," she snores like a porpoise, and she too would rule her husband with her "masculine and loud commanding." Morose exclaims the minute after he is married, "She is my regent already!" To escape from this trap, Morose would geld himself, and he confesses before all assembled, "I am no man . . . utterly unabled in nature, by reason of frigidity, to perform the duties or any the least office of a husband." So he becomes a "bridegroom uncarnate." Finally he even thanks the knights for proving him a cuckold.

Although each of these characters puts up a façade of sensibility, courage, sexual prowess, fashion, family, language, or learning, trying to impress the world, it only makes us question what is behind their act. The job of Truewit is twofold: to inspire wit in others and to penetrate appearances, vex the fool and hypocrite until they reveal their essential hollowness. "Why, all their actions are governed by crude opinion, without reason or cause; they know not why they do anything but as they are inform'd, believe, judge, praise, condemn, love, hate, and in emulation one of another, do all these things alike. Only, they have a natural inclination [that] sways 'em generally to the worst, when they are left to themselves." Appropriately, Truewit enjoys putting words in other people's mouths. As Northrop Frye has suggested, comedy usually aims to "cure" the blocking characters or to cast them out of comic society. So Truewit's vexations, his "excellent comedy of affliction," isolate and test the true worth of characters, to show they are not worthy of society. Beneath their noise, their bad poetry, pretentious genealogy, false fashion, and affected language, the fools are shown to be empty. But there are so many of them, and they are so incurably ignorant that all cannot be cast out. Daw and La Foole go, displaced by Dauphine and Clerimont, but the rest must be tolerated, manipulated, and "taken."

Morose, however, is another case. Beneath his egotistic jabbering there lurks a sadist, a hater of mankind, fearful of any sounds of life itself, whose distended imagination gloats over the possible sufferings of Dauphine (II.v), just as Sir Epicure Mammon's diseased mind conjures up grotesque sensual pleasures. Morose would have survived well enough if he had remained faithful to his retiring humor and if he had been content to dominate his own little household, but he suspected Dauphine and he would revenge himself, extending himself beyond his humor into marriage. Like Volpone, he has more to his character than a single passion or affectation, and it is the complication of his personality that gets him into trouble. When Morose steps out of his humor, he increases his foolishness and turns willingly to his own destruction. His early speeches seem calculated to alienate the sympathies of an audience, and Jonson was careful to keep him as rigid and mechanical as possible, speaking through a tube, demanding bows, wearing caps and flourishing swords—not a medical case but a social monster. If Morose had remained on stage through Acts IV and V constantly suffering, perhaps he would have attracted some pity, but Jonson depends more upon off-stage reports of his agony. Then he comes forth when he must humiliate himself before the assembly. Yet even here Jonson mitigates the punishment; after all, Morose escapes from the incredible mismatch with Epicoene, and he willingly seeks to be left alone to die in peaceful silence (back in his simple humor); like other Renaissance panteloons, Shylock and Malvolio, he is too unregenerate for a community of living, though hollow, men.

The plan, then, of the whole play is a tissue of afflictions visited upon hermaphroditical monsters, an elaborate game of vexation copiously filled with variety. As Jonson remarked in *Timber*, a sufficient plot should expand as far as possible within the bounds of art "and every bound, for the nature of the subject, is esteemed the best that is largest, till it can increase no more: so it behoves the action in

tragedy or comedy to bè let grow, till necessity ask a conclusion"
(ed. H.S., VIII, 646–647). Much of the play is like the working out
of a series of permutations with a fixed number of constants and two
variables: what are the maximum number of combinations of
character and situation that can be represented on the stage without
repeating a single pattern? Or like change ringing of church bells
that became popular in the early seventeenth century: societies
were founded, one of them in London called the College Youths,
and urbane gentlemen got together to ring the changes. Five bells,
they discovered, could be rung 120 "plain" changes without repeti-
tion of their order, six bells 720 times, and seven bells 5,040 times.
The passion was for completeness and variety, within fixed limits.[9]
As in the pursuit of a wench "variety arrests . . . judgment" (IV.i.58),
so the typical Jonsonian plot, once it fixes on a significant pattern,
gives the illusion of working out a variety of possible combinations.

This is different from Shakespeare's mode of construction, which is
more open-ended, aiming for a more complete range of experience,
like the world itself. Jonson chooses a little world, represented by a
large but circumscribed cast. They are Londoners who might come
in contact with the fashionable gentry and who are afflicted with a
similar social disease. Gradations are clearly marked between servants,
pretenders, and collegiates; between womanish men, mannish
women, lusty men, insatiable women, and an impotent old man.
Jonson has strictly limited the time: one crucial day during the
plague when Morose has determined to marry. He has limited the
place: the fashionable district between Westminster and the City of
London, near the Strand, the Law Courts, and the Thames, in short,
near the Whitefriars Theatre. And he has controlled the plot, allowing
it to rise by gradual degrees of complication and furor, developed by
an incredible series of reciprocities. It is like an expandable filing
system into which an indeterminate number of set speeches, characters, and episodes can be inserted, as long as the cross references are
complete. At first only two or three characters come together to
irritate each other; then four, five, and soon the stage is filled. At the
first climax, in Act III, the mob washes onto the stage in three waves.
Then, in separate episodes, Mr. Otter begins on Mrs. Otter and
in the same action belittles the knights for their timid drinking;
the ladies work on Morose's melancholy, in a parody of learned

9 See J. J. Raven, *The Bells of England* (1906), pp. 229–246, for a brief
description of change ringing.

disputation over ancient versus modern writers; finally, Daw is set
at odds with La Foole.

This second series is linked in two ways: by the noise each creates to
irritate Morose and by the rising challenge to Truewit's ingenuity.
Can he make the ladies dote on Dauphine before the night is over?
Efficiency becomes the watchword. He improvises brilliantly and
makes the play within the play, the tragicomedy of Daw and La
Foole, serve as entertainment to the College, but allows the credit
to go to Dauphine. In the third climax Cutbeard and Otter double as
the civil and canon lawyers, exploiting their linguistic pretensions,
showing that a garment and a few "terms" are enough to make a
lawyer. All of this vexes Morose further, in some elaborate casuistic
disputation that seems overdone in the reading, but it works on the
stage.[10] The game of vexation has become a "waking dream"
(IV.vii.41), and at the pitch of excitement Morose exclaims, "Oh,
the variety and changes of my torment!" (V.iv.9).

Jonson apparently believed that he needed something bigger than
the charade of the fourth act, something with suspense, to precede
the final surprise. With the entire cast assembled for the first time, at
Truewit's highest moment, he maneuvers Morose into his lacerating
confession: "I am no man, ladies." It is Clerimont's finest moment
when he forces Daw and La Foole to brag about their conquests of
Epicoene, but in the final unmasking Dauphine exposes everyone.

The total effect seems somehow equivocal. The series of brilliant
set speeches so thoroughly attack polite learning, feminine beauty,
art, marriage, and fashion that urbane life appears to be little worth
all the effort to live it. Dauphine himself shows less wit than cruelty.
He would as soon take off Daw's arm or tweak off La Foole's nose.
Truewit has to restrain him both times: "How! Maim a man forever
for a jest? What a conscience hast thou?" In the process of making the
Collegiates admire Dauphine, Truewit shows their shallow minds—
a reflection on Clerimont and Dauphine's taste. Furthermore, as
each of the gulls vies with himself to aid in his public humiliation, we
see Jonson trying for maximum irony, to have a character convinced
that he will personally profit by some degrading act, only to fall
deeper into self-deception and frustration. Such turns, although
expertly carried off, finally drain a character of his last ounce of
humanity. We can laugh callously and cast him aside, but the net

[10] See James Agate's review of the performance November 18, 1924:
Brief Chronicles (1943), pp. 79–80.

effect is to leave us troubled. Some deep cynicism, some reserve of self-mockery, of loathing and contempt, seems to lurk beneath the dazzling artifice of the play:

> it is to be presum'd,
> Though art's hid causes are not found,
> All is not sweet, all is not sound.[11]

DATE AND TEXT

Considerable uncertainty surrounds the publishing of *Epicoene* because the facts are difficult to interpret. Since the Venetian ambassador's letter (cited above), in which the play's suppression was mentioned, dates from February 8, 1609/10, we may assume that some version of *Epicoene* was acted before that time. The title page of the first edition in the 1616 folio of *The Workes of Benjamin Jonson* gives only the year 1609:

EPICŒNE,/ OR/ The silent Woman./ *A Comœdie.*/ Acted in the yeere 1609. By/ the Children of her Maiesties/ REVELLS./ The Author B. I./ HORAT./ *Vt sis tu similis Cælí, Byrrhíą, lątronum,/ Non ego sim Caprí, neą, Sulcí. Cur metuas me?*/ [rule]/ LONDON,/ Printed by WILLIAM STANSBY./ [rule]/ M. DC. XVI.

But we know that the Children's company could not have opened at the Whitefriars Theatre until deaths from the plague fell below forty per week.[12] In 1609 there were 4,240 deaths recorded in the London

---

[11] Further discussion can be found in Jonas A. Barish, *Ben Jonson and the Language of Prose Comedy* (1960); Edmund Wilson's "Morose Ben Jonson," in *The Triple Thinkers* (revised ed., 1948), reprinted in *Ben Jonson: A Collection of Critical Essays*, ed. Barish (1963). For comment on hermaphroditism see Edward B. Partridge, *The Broken Compass: A Study of the Major Comedies of Ben Jonson* (1958); the chapter on *Epicoene* is reprinted in Barish's collection. Ray L. Heffner, Jr., "Unifying Symbols in the Comedy of Ben Jonson," from *English Stage Comedy*, ed. W. K. Wimsatt, Jr. (1955), reprinted in Barish's collection, has some provocative remarks on plot. Sources are discussed by O. J. Campbell, "The Relation of *Epicoene* to Aretino's *Il Marescalco*," *PMLA*, XLVI (1931), 752–762, and by Jonas Barish in a good article, "Ovid, Juvenal, and *The Silent Woman*," *PMLA*, LXXI (1956), 213–224. James D. Redwine, Jr., "Beyond Psychology: The Moral Basis of Jonson's Theory of Humour Characterization," *Journal of English Literary History*, XXVIII (1961), 316–334, corrects some common errors.

[12] See F. P. Wilson, *The Plague in Shakespeare's London*, rev. ed. (1963), p. 125.

area, but the week ending December 7 reached a low of only thirty-odd deaths. This circumstance limits the run of *Epicoene* to a period between December 7, 1609, and early February 1609/10. (The legal year began on Lady Day, March 25, although people celebrated New Year's Day on January 1.)

Jonson may have intended early publication, for an entry survives in the Register of the Stationers' Company, September 20, 1610:

> John Browne John Busby *junior/* Entred for their copye under thandes of Sir George Bucke and master Waterson for master warden Leake, A booke called, *Epicoene or the silent woman* by
> BEN: JOHNSON   [ed. Arber, III, 444]

In the same register, on September 28, 1612 (III, 498) Browne transferred his rights to Walter Burre, a bookseller who owned the rights to six other Jonson plays; and presumably he received some private compensation for the use of the plays in the folio. Stansby did not buy him out until 1621 (the transaction recorded in 1635, when Stansby planned the second folio).

I do not believe that any separate edition of the play ever appeared until 1620. Contrary to much speculation, I think that D. E. Baker, who claimed there was a 1609 quarto,[13] and William Gifford, who said he saw a quarto of 1612, were mistaken. The resources of our great modern libraries contain no such book, but it seems especially suspicious that Gifford cites no variants from 1612, as he usually did in other cases. W. W. Greg suggested that Francis Beaumont's verses appended to the 1616 folio may have been prepared for some earlier publication of *Epicoene*. If he had to make a choice Greg thought it should be in favor of a 1612 quarto.[14] However, Professor J. Gerritsen's study,[15] duplicated by me, of the play's folio printing revealed some new evidence. The printer had considerable difficulty with his copy, and the first twelve pages of text (gathering 2Y6, affecting the prologues and I.i.1 to II.ii.59) had to be scrapped after an uncertain number of sheets had gone through the press. Apparently Jonson or the master printer saw numerous errors and omissions. Daw's and Dauphine's speech prefixes were hopelessly confused

13 *Companion to the Playhouse* (1764), II, 200 (1812 edition).
14 "Was there a 1612 Quarto of *Epicoene*?" *Library*, 4th series, XV (1935), 306–315.
15 See J. Gerritsen, "Stansby and Jonson Produce a Folio: A Preliminary Account," *English Studies*, XL (1959), 52–55.

because the abbreviation DAV. was too much like DAW. Only the large paper copies have the earlier setting of 2Y^6, and the small paper copies (as well as one large paper copy in the Sheffield University Library) have the resetting. Gerritsen designates them, more precisely, as the "common" and the "rare" settings. The resetting shows obvious authorial revisions such as *marching* replacing *going* (I.i.168) and *preachings* replacing *parleys* (II.ii.32); and at least thirteen corrections, seven additions, and one error—*Thy* for *They* at I.i.96.

Simpson was unquestionably wrong when he concluded that the small paper sheets of this gathering were original settings and the large paper were careless resettings. He may have been influenced by the assumption that large paper went through the press after small paper, because large paper copies usually contain later states of the press corrections of the folio. At any rate, a break in the border of an ornamental "T" (sig. 2Y1) and changes in the headlines offer incontrovertible proof that existing small paper of 2Y is the resetting. Roughly the same skeleton formes were reused in subsequent formes, and the headlines show gradual shifting and some damage, in a progression from 2Y (large paper), 2Z, 3A–3D, 2Y (small paper). Hence the formes of 2Y (small paper) were imposed and printed after the entire play had been run off. But at some time after the large paper sheets (and possibly a full printing of small paper sheets, later destroyed) of 2Y came off the press, Jonson restyled the copy so that Dauphine's speeches could be distinguished from Daw's, although he missed a number of prefixes. At the same time he could have made the revisions, contrary to his claim in the already printed Dedication ("There is not a line or syllable in it changed from the simplicity of the first copy").

If the copy had been a printed quarto, we would expect these difficulties to have been ironed out in the first printing. Consequently, I agree with Gerritsen that a manuscript was probably used for copy. Hence there never was a 1612 quarto. For if some earlier quarto had been suppressed, we might expect that at least the author or bookseller kept one book to use later.

Two other sheets, 2X1.6 and 3A1.6, were reset after the printing of the entire book, probably in order to make up shortages, so they contain no authoritative alterations, merely corruptions (affecting the Dedication, Cast of Characters, III.i.18 to III.ii.61, and III.vi.60 to III.vii.43). Neither does Jonson appear to have had any direct or indirect responsibility for the quarto of 1620, whose title page (dubbed in after the first one was canceled) used the more popular name for the play: *The Silent Woman*. The second folio (1640) was set from a copy of 1616, and the third folio (1692) was set from the second. Therefore the first folio in its various states is the sole authority for the text.

The present edition is faithful to the wording of the folio, except where noted, and it follows the reset version of 2Y⁶, save for two readings, but it follows the original settings of 2X1.6 and 3A1.6. Certain anonymous early manuscript corrections in copy six at the Folger Shakespeare Library clarify a few passages, but most of them agree with obvious corrections made in Q, F2, and F3. Collations by machine of twelve copies of F1 (eight Folger, three Library of Congress, and one University of Virginia) revealed a few more press corrections than Simpson found; only two of them were substantive however, and they are recorded in the notes. In the Appendix, along with readings from derivative seventeenth-century editions, I have noted some interesting variations from two previously uncollated manuscripts of "Still to be neat." The linked variants in the Folger manuscript suggest that it is another version, definitely inferior to the printed text, possibly an early draft such as we know of "Drink to me only with thine eyes."

I have preserved the continental style of act and scene division that Jonson preferred, but have removed the names of characters from "massed" entries and inserted them within brackets at the point where they should enter. A footnote in each case records the form of the original entry. Jonson's marginal stage directions have been silently incorporated into the text with parentheses; most of the bracketed directions were first introduced by Gifford, although he is not mentioned in the apparatus unless I disagree with his choice.

I am grateful for the permission of the Clarendon Press to use a number of explanatory notes from the Oxford edition. But I have redone the text entirely from the original editions, because, sad to say, Herford and Simpson's text contains some errors, partly due to their mistaken view of the resetting of sig. 2Y and partly to their evident use of Miss A. Henry's doctoral dissertation for printer's copy (Yale Studies in English, Vol. XXXI, 1906). Errors that are found only in Miss Henry's text reappear embarrassingly often in the Herford and Simpson edition; for example, see entries in Appendix A for IV.ii.13, IV.v.90, and IV.vi.98 (my lineation). I am indebted to Professor Gerritsen for reading and criticizing my textual introduction. I thank the Folger Library, Dr. James McManaway, and Miss Elizabeth Niemyer for their help when I spent three months in Washington on a Folger Fellowship. I am indebted to several of my students for suggestions for the notes, and especially to Mr. Anderson Orr.

L. A. BEAURLINE

University of Virginia

EPICOENE

or

THE SILENT WOMAN

To the Truly Noble, By All Titles, Sir Francis Stuart:

S<small>IR</small>,

    My hope is not so nourish'd by example, as it will con-
clude this dumb piece should please you by cause it hath
pleas'd others before, but by trust that when you have read   5
it, you will find it worthy to have displeas'd none. This
makes that I now number you not only in the names of favor
but the names of justice to what I write, and do presently
call you to the exercise of that noblest and manliest virtue,
as coveting rather to be freed in my fame by the authority   10
of a judge than the credit of an undertaker. Read therefore, I
pray you, and censure. There is not a line or syllable in it
changed from the simplicity of the first copy. And, when
you shall consider, through the certain hatred of some, how
much a man's innocency may be endanger'd by an uncer-   15
tain accusation, you will, I doubt not, so begin to hate the
iniquity of such natures as I shall love the contumely done
me, whose end was so honorable as to be wip'd off by your
sentence.

                    Your unprofitable but true lover,   20

                          B<small>EN</small> J<small>ONSON</small>

---

    1. *Sir Francis Stuart*] "a learned gentleman, and one of the club at the
Mermaid . . . with Sir Walter Ralegh, etc., of that sodality: heros and wits
of that time" (Aubrey, ii, 239).
    11. *undertaker*] guarantor.

PROLOGUE

Truth says of old the art of making plays
   Was to content the people, and their praise
   Was to the Poet money, wine, and bays.
But in this age a sect of writers are,
   That only for particular likings care   5
   And will taste nothing that is popular.
With such we mingle neither brains nor breasts;
   Our wishes, like to those make public feasts,
   Are not to please the cooks' tastes but the guests'.
Yet if those cunning palates hither come,   10
   They shall find guests' entreaty and good room;
   And though all relish not, sure there will be some
That, when they leave their seats, shall make 'em say,
   Who wrote that piece could so have wrote a play,
   But that he knew this was the better way.   15
For to present all custard or all tart
   And have no other meats to bear a part,
   Or to want bread and salt, were but coarse art.
The Poet prays you then with better thought
   To sit, and when his cates are all in brought,   20
   Though there be none far fet, there will dear-bought
Be fit for ladies, some for lords, knights, squires,
   Some for your waiting-wench, and city-wires,
   Some for your men, and daughters of Whitefriars.
Nor is it only while you keep your seat   25
   Here that his feast will last, but you shall eat
   A week at ord'naries on his broken meat,

8. make . . . feasts] *F1* (*orig.*); (make
. . . feasts) *F1* (*reset*).

---

  11. *entreaty*] entertainment.
  20. *cates*] choice foods.
  21. *far fet*] imported. "Far fet and dear bought is good for ladies" (John Lyly, *Euphues*, ed. Arber, 1895, p. 93).
  23. *city-wires*] citizen's wives who aped the fashions. Wires supported hair and ruffs.
  24. *daughters of Whitefriars*] according to Lady Wouldbe, hermaphrodite ladies, who dress in men's clothes, come from Whitefriars (*Volpone*, IV.ii.51).
  27. *ord'naries*] taverns that serve meals.

If his muse be true
Who commends her to you.

Another:
Occasion'd by some person's impertinent exception.

The ends of all who for the scene do write
  Are or should be to profit and delight.
And still't hath been the praise of all best times,
  So persons were not touch'd, to tax the crimes.
Then in this play which we present tonight   5
  And make the object of your ear and sight,
On forfeit of yourselves, think nothing true,
  Lest so you make the maker to judge you.
For he knows poet never credit gain'd
  By writing truths, but things (like truths) well feign'd.   10
If any yet will, with particular sleight
  Of application, wrest what he doth write
And that he meant or him or her will say,
  They make a libel which he made a play.

0.1 *Occasion'd . . . exception*] *marginal
note F1 (reset); om. F1 (orig.).*

---

8. *the maker*] the poet.

THE PERSONS OF THE PLAY

MOROSE, *a gentleman that loves no noise*
[SIR] DAUPHINE EUGENIE, *a knight, his nephew*
[NED] CLERIMONT, *a gentleman, his friend*
TRUEWIT, *another friend*
EPICOENE, *a young gentleman suppos'd the silent woman*   5
[SIR] JOHN DAW, *a knight, her servant*
[SIR] AMOROUS LA FOOLE, *a knight also*
TOM OTTER, *a land and sea captain*
CUTBEARD, *a barber*
MUTE, *one of Morose his servants*   10
MADAME HAUGHTY ⎱
MADAME CENTAUR ⎰ *Ladies Collegiates*
MISTRESS [DOL] MAVIS ⎰
MISTRESS TRUSTY, *the Lady Haughty's woman* ⎱ *Pretenders*   15
MISTRESS OTTER, *the captain's wife* ⎰
PARSON, PAGES, SERVANTS

The Scene, *London*

15. *Pretenders*] see note below.

---

1. *Morose*] The Latin *morosus* means "wayward, froward, hard to please: more curious or hard than need" (Cooper).
12. *Collegiates*] members of a fellowship. Jonson probably refers to women's literary salons. The Countess of Pembroke's was called a "college" (Aubrey).
15. *Pretenders*] The arrangement of ll. 14–16 in F1 is such that "Pretenders" seems to refer only to Mistress Otter:

MISTRESS TRUSTY.	*The Lady Haughty's woman.*
MISTRESS OTTER.	*The Captain's wife.* {*Pretenders.*

Jonson probably intended that "Pretenders" should refer to Mistress Trusty and Mistress Otter, but the printer did not have enough room to insert a brace including lines 14–16.

Epicoene, or The Silent Woman

Ut sis tu similis Caeli, Byrrhique latronum,
Non ego sim Capri, neque Sulci. Cur metuas me?
                                                    Horat.

[I.i]
[*Enter*] Clerimont: *he comes out making himself ready,* [*followed by*] Boy.

CLERIMONT.

Ha' you got the song yet perfect I ga' you, boy?

BOY.

Yes, sir.

CLERIMONT.

Let me hear it.

BOY.

You shall, sir, but i' faith let nobody else.

CLERIMONT.

Why, I pray?   5

BOY.

It will get you the dangerous name of a poet in town, sir,
besides me a perfect deal of ill-will at the mansion you wot
of, whose lady is the argument of it, where now I am the
welcom'st thing under a man that comes there.

CLERIMONT.

I think, and above a man too, if the truth were rack'd out   10
of you.

0.1.] Clerimont, Boy, Truewit. *F1*.

Ut ... me?] Epigraph from the title page, 1616. "Though you may be
like highwaymen, Coelus and Byrrhus, I am not [a common slanderer] like
Caprius and Sulcius. Why should you be afraid of me?" (Horace *Satires*
I.iv.69–70).

6. *dangerous ... poet*] because poets satirize folly, and in society it was "a
most contemptible nick name" (*Timber*, ed. H. S., VIII, 572).

BOY.

No, faith, I'll confess before, sir. The gentlewomen play
with me and throw me o' the bed, and carry me in to my
lady, and she kisses me with her oil'd face and puts a peruke
o' my head and asks me an' I will wear her gown, and I say,   15
"No." And then she hits me a blow o' the ear and calls me
innocent and lets me go.

CLERIMONT.

No marvel if the door be kept shut against your master,
when the entrance is so easy to you— Well sir, you shall
go there no more, lest I be fain to seek your voice in my   20
lady's rushes a fortnight hence. Sing, sir.   *Boy sings.*

[*Enter* Truewit.]

TRUEWIT.

Why, here's the man that can melt away his time, and
never feels it! What between his mistress abroad and his
ingle at home, high fare, soft lodging, fine clothes, and his
fiddle, he thinks the hours ha' no wings or the day no post   25
horse. Well, sir gallant, were you strook with the plague
this minute or condemn'd to any capital punishment tomorrow, you would begin then to think and value every
article o' your time, esteem it at the true rate and give all
for't.   30

CLERIMONT.

Why, what should a man do?

TRUEWIT.

Why, nothing, or that which when 'tis done is as idle.
Harken after the next horse race or hunting match; lay
wagers, praise Puppy, or Peppercorn, Whitefoot, Franklin;
swear upon Whitemane's party; spend aloud that my lords   35
may hear you; visit my ladies at night and be able to give
'em the character of every bowler or bettor o' the green.

---

21. *Boy sings*] *Page sings.* Still to be   34.] *F1 (reset) contains marginal note,*
neat, still to be drest—*Gifford.*   "Horses o' the time," *om. F1 (orig.).*

---

   21. *rushes*] strewn on the floor.
   24. *ingle*] catamite, boy.
   26. *strook*] struck.
   35. *spend aloud*] speak or sound aloud, as hounds bark when they see the
game.

These be the things wherein your fashionable men exercise
themselves, and I for company.

CLERIMONT.

Nay, if I have thy authority, I'll not leave yet. Come, the   40
other are considerations when we come to have gray heads
and weak hams, moist eyes and shrunk members. We'll
think on 'em then; then we'll pray and fast.

TRUEWIT.

Ay, and destine only that time of age to goodness, which
our want of ability will not let us employ in evil?   45

CLERIMONT.

Why then 'tis time enough.

TRUEWIT.

Yes, as if a man should sleep all the term and think to
effect his business the last day. Oh, Clerimont, this time,
because it is an incorporeal thing and not subject to sense,
we mock ourselves the fineliest out of it, with vanity and   50
misery indeed, not seeking an end of wretchedness but
only changing the matter still.

CLERIMONT.

Nay, thou'lt not leave now—

TRUEWIT.

See but our common disease! With what justice can we
complain that great men will not look upon us nor be at   55
leisure to give our affairs such dispatch as we expect, when
we will never do it to ourselves, nor hear nor regard ourselves.

CLERIMONT.

Foh, thou hast read Plutarch's *Morals* now, or some such
tedious fellow, and it shows so vilely with thee, 'fore God,   60
'twill spoil thy wit utterly. Talk me of pins and feathers and
ladies and rushes and such things, and leave this stoicity
alone till thou mak'st sermons.

57. nor hear] *F1* (*reset*); not hear
F1 (*orig.*).

---

40. *leave*] leave off.
47. *term*] the period during which cases could be tried in law courts.
54. *common disease*] discontent because of lack of patronage, causing
melancholy.
60. *tedious fellow*] the stoic philosopher, Seneca, *De Brevitate Vitae*, iii, 5,
paraphrased in ll. 48–52 (H.S.).

TRUEWIT.

    Well, sir, if it will not take, I have learn'd to lose as little
of my kindness as I can. I'll do good to no man against his   65
will, certainly. When were you at the college?

CLERIMONT.

    What college?

TRUEWIT.

    As if you knew not!

CLERIMONT.

    No, faith, I came but from court yesterday.

TRUEWIT.

    Why, is it not arriv'd there yet, the news? A new founda-   70
tion, sir, here i' the town, of ladies that call themselves the
collegiates, an order between courtiers and country madams,
that live from their husbands and give entertainment to all
the Wits and Braveries o' the time, as they call 'em, cry down
or up what they like or dislike in a brain or a fashion with   75
most masculine or rather hermaphroditical authority, and
every day gain to their college some new probationer.

CLERIMONT.

    Who is the president?

TRUEWIT.

    The grave and youthful matron, the Lady Haughty.

CLERIMONT.

    A pox of her autumnal face, her piec'd beauty. There's no   80
man can be admitted till she be ready nowadays, till she has
painted and perfum'd and wash'd and scour'd, but the boy
here, and him she wipes her oil'd lips upon like a sponge.
I have made a song, I pray thee hear it, o' the subject.

                                            [Boy *sings again.*]

SONG

             Still to be neat, still to be dress'd,   85
             As you were going to a feast;

64. Well, sir,] Well, sir. *F1.*   82. scour'd] *F1* (*reset*); sour'd *F1*
                                                     (*orig.*).

---

   74. *Wits and Braveries*] fashionable cliques of gallants (H.S.).
   85–96.] See Appendix A for readings from a possibly early draft of this
song.

Still to be powder'd, still perfum'd:
Lady, it is to be presum'd,
Though art's hid causes are not found,
All is not sweet, all is not sound.   90

Give me a look, give me a face,
That makes simplicity a grace;
Robes loosely flowing, hair as free:
Such sweet neglect more taketh me,
Than all th' adulteries of art.   95
They strike mine eyes, but not my heart.

TRUEWIT.

And I am clearly o' the other side: I love a good dressing
before any beauty o' the world. Oh, a woman is then like a
delicate garden; nor is there one kind of it: she may vary
every hour, take often counsel of her glass and choose the 100
best. If she have good ears, shew 'em; good hair, lay it
out; good legs, wear short clothes; a good hand, discover it
often; practice any art to mend breath, cleanse teeth, repair
eyebrows, paint, and profess it.

CLERIMONT.

How, publicly?   105

TRUEWIT.

The doing of it, not the manner: that must be private.
Many things that seem foul i' the doing, do please, done.
A lady should indeed study her face when we think she
sleeps; nor when the doors are shut should men be inquiring;
all is sacred within then. Is it for us to see their perukes put 110
on, their false teeth, their complexion, their eyebrows, their
nails? You see gilders will not work but enclos'd. They must
not discover how little serves with the help of art to adorn
a great deal. How long did the canvas hang afore Aldgate?
Were the people suffer'd to see the city's *Love* and *Charity* 115
while they were rude stone, before they were painted and

96. They] *F1* (*orig.*); Thy *F1*
(*reset*).

95. *adulteries*] adulteration.
114. *Aldgate*] one of the old city gates, decorated with two statues.

burnish'd? No. No more should servants approach their
mistresses but when they are complete and finish'd.

CLERIMONT.

Well said, my Truewit.

TRUEWIT.

And a wise lady will keep a guard always upon the place, 120
that she may do things securely. I once followed a rude
fellow into a chamber, where the poor madam, for haste,
and troubled, snatch'd at her peruke to cover her baldness
and put it on the wrong way.

CLERIMONT.

Oh prodigy!   125

TRUEWIT.

And the unconscionable knave held her in compliment an
hour, with that revers'd face, when I still look'd when she
should talk from the t'other side.

CLERIMONT.

Why, thou should'st ha' reliev'd her.

TRUEWIT.

No faith, I let her alone as we'll let this argument, if you 130
please, and pass to another. When saw you Dauphine
Eugenie?

CLERIMONT.

Not these three days. Shall we go to him this morning? He
is very melancholic, I hear.

TRUEWIT.

Sick o' the uncle, is he? I met that stiff piece of formality, 135
his uncle, yesterday, with a huge turbant of nightcaps on
his head, buckled over his ears.

CLERIMONT.

Oh, that's his custom when he walks abroad. He can endure
no noise, man.

TRUEWIT.

So I have heard. But is the disease so ridiculous in him as it 140
is made? They say he has been upon divers treaties with the
fishwives and orange-women, and articles propounded

---

117. *servants*] submissive lovers in the ritual of courtly love.
136. *turbant*] turban.
142. *orange-women*] who cried their wares in the streets.

between them. Marry, the chimney-sweepers will not be
drawn in.

CLERIMONT.

No, nor the broom-men: they stand out stiffly. He cannot   145
endure a costardmonger, he swoons if he hear one.

TRUEWIT.

Methinks a smith should be ominous.

CLERIMONT.

Or any hammerman. A brasier is not suffer'd to dwell in
the parish, nor an armorer. He would have hang'd a
pewterer's 'prentice once upon a Shrove-Tuesday's riot for   150
being o' that trade, when the rest were quit.

TRUEWIT.

A trumpet should fright him terribly, or the hautboys?

CLERIMONT.

Out of his senses. The waits of the city have a pension of
him not to come near that ward. This youth practic'd on
him one night like the bellman, and never left till he had   155
brought him down to the door with a long sword, and there
left him flourishing with the air.

BOY.

Why, sir, he hath chosen a street to lie in so narrow at
both ends that it will receive no coaches nor carts nor any
of these common noises, and therefore we that love him   160
devise to bring him in such as we may, now and then, for
his exercise, to breathe him. He would grow resty else in his
ease. His virtue would rust without action. I entreated a
bearward one day to come down with the dogs of some four
parishes that way, and I thank him he did, and cried his   165
games under Master Morose's windore till he was sent

150. upon] up on *F1 (reset)*; on *F1*   158. sir,] sir! *F1 (reset)*; sir? *F1*
(orig.).   *(orig.)*.
                                             161. in] *F1 (reset)*; om. *F1 (orig.)*.

---

143. *chimney-sweepers*] who sang "Soot—Sweep—O" (Henry).
146. *costardmonger*] fruitseller.
150. *Shrove-Tuesday's riot*] when apprentices wrecked brothels and
playhouses.
153. *waits*] street musicians.
155. *bellman*] night watchman.   162. *resty*] lazy.
164. *bearward*] trainer of bears.   166. *windore*] window.

crying away with his head made a most bleeding spectacle
to the multitude. And another time a fencer, marching to his
prize, had his drum most tragically run through for taking
that street in his way, at my request.   170

TRUEWIT.

A good wag. How does he for the bells?

CLERIMONT.

Oh, i' the Queen's time he was wont to go out of town
every Saturday at ten o'clock or on holiday eves. But now
by reason of the sickness, the perpetuity of ringing has made
him devise a room with double walls, and treble ceilings, the 175
windores close shut and caulk'd, and there he lives by
candlelight. He turn'd away a man last week for having
a pair of new shoes that creak'd. And this fellow waits on
him now in tennis-court socks, or slippers sol'd with wool,
and they talk each to other in a trunk. See who comes here. 180

[I.ii]   [*Enter*] Dauphine.

DAUPHINE.

How now! What ail you sirs? Dumb?

TRUEWIT.

Strook into stone almost, I am here, with tales o' thine
uncle! There was never such a prodigy heard of.

DAUPHINE.

I would you would once lose this subject, my masters, for
my sake. They are such as you are that have brought me   5
into that predicament I am with him.

TRUEWIT.

How is that?

DAUPHINE.

Marry, that he will disinherit me, no more. He thinks I

---

168. marching] *F1 (reset)*; going *F1*
(*orig.*).

[I.ii]
0.1.] Dauphine, Truewit, Clerimont. *F1*.
4. lose] *F2–3*; loose *F1*.

---

169. *prize*] match.
174. *ringing*] tolling church bells for the dead. In some parishes the
passing bell never stopped during the plague of 1609.
180. *a trunk*] speaking tube.

and my company are authors of all the ridiculous acts and
monuments are told of him.   10

TRUEWIT.

'Slid, I would be the author of more to vex him; that
purpose deserves it: it gives thee law of plaguing him.
I'll tell thee what I would do. I would make a false almanac,
get it printed, and then ha' him drawn out on a coronation
day to the Tower Wharf, and kill him with the noise of   15
the ordnance. Disinherit thee! He cannot, man. Art not thou
next of blood, and his sister's son?

DAUPHINE.

Ay, but he will thrust me out of it, he vows, and marry.

TRUEWIT.

How! That's a more portent. Can he endure no noise, and
will venture on a wife?   20

CLERIMONT.

Yes. Why, thou art a stranger, it seems, to his best trick
yet. He has employed a fellow this half year all over England
to harken him out a dumb woman, be she of any form or
any quality, so she be able to bear children. Her silence is
dowry enough, he says.   25

TRUEWIT.

But I trust to God he has found none.

CLERIMONT.

No, but he has heard of one that's lodg'd i' the next street
to him, who is exceedingly soft-spoken, thrifty of her speech,
that spends but six words a day. And her he's about now
and shall have her.   30

TRUEWIT.

Is't possible! Who is his agent i' the business?

CLERIMONT.

Marry, a barber, one Cutbeard, an honest fellow, one that
tells Dauphine all here.

10. monuments] moniments *F1*.   32. one Cutbeard] *F1* (*reset*); *om. F1*
21. Yes.] Yes: *F1* (*reset*); Yes, *F1*   (*orig.*).
(*orig.*).

9–10. *acts and monuments*] John Foxe's popular "Book of Martyrs" was
entitled *Actes and Monuments* (1563).
   15. *Tower Wharf*] where gunfire celebrated the anniversary of the King's
coronation, on the bank of the Thames close by the Tower of London.
   19. *more*] more serious.

TRUEWIT.

> Why, you oppress me with wonder! A woman and a barber,
> and love no noise!   35

CLERIMONT.

> Yes, faith. The fellow trims him silently and has not the
> knack with his shears or his fingers, and that continence in
> a barber he thinks so eminent a virtue as it has made him
> chief of his counsel.

TRUEWIT.

> Is the barber to be seen, or the wench?   40

CLERIMONT.

> Yes, that they are.

TRUEWIT.

> I pray thee, Dauphine, let's go thither.

DAUPHINE.

> I have some business now; I cannot i' faith.

TRUEWIT.

> You shall have no business shall make you neglect this, sir.
> We'll make her talk, believe it; or if she will not, we can   45
> give out at least so much as shall interrupt the treaty. We
> will break it. Thou art bound in conscience, when he
> suspects thee without cause, to torment him.

DAUPHINE.

> Not I, by any means. I'll give no suffrage to't. He shall never
> ha' that plea against me that I oppos'd the least fant'sy of   50
> his. Let it lie upon my stars to be guilty, I'll be innocent.

TRUEWIT.

> Yes, and be poor and beg; do, innocent, when some groom
> of his has got him an heir, or this barber, if he himself
> cannot. Innocent! —I pray thee, Ned, where lies she? Let
> him be innocent still.   55

CLERIMONT.

> Why, right over against the barber's, in the house where
> Sir John Daw lies.

TRUEWIT.

> You do not mean to confound me!

---

37. *fingers*] a barber could "snap his fingers with dexterity" (*Green's
Tu Quoque*, in *Dodsley's Old Plays*, ed. Hazlitt, XI, 210).
   51. *my stars*] my fate.

CLERIMONT.

    Why?

TRUEWIT.

    Does he that would marry her know so much?   60

CLERIMONT.

    I cannot tell.

TRUEWIT.

    'Twere enough of imputation to her, with him.

CLERIMONT.

    Why?

TRUEWIT.

    The only talking sir i'th' town! Jack Daw! And he teach
    her not to speak—God b'w'you. I have some business too.   65

CLERIMONT.

    Will you not go thither then?

TRUEWIT.

    Not with the danger to meet Daw, for mine ears.

CLERIMONT.

    Why, I thought you two had been upon very good terms.

TRUEWIT.

    Yes, of keeping distance.

CLERIMONT.

    They say he is a very good scholar.   70

TRUEWIT.

    Ay, and he says it first. A pox on him, a fellow that pretends
    only to learning, buys titles, and nothing else of books in
    him.

CLERIMONT.

    The world reports him to be very learned.

TRUEWIT.

    I am sorry the world should so conspire to belie him.   75

CLERIMONT.

    Good faith, I have heard very good things come from him.

TRUEWIT.

    You may. There's none so desperately ignorant to deny
    that: would they were his own. God b'w'you gentlemen.

CLERIMONT.

    This is very abrupt.   [*Exit* Truewit.]

---

62. *to her*] against her.

[I.iii]

DAUPHINE.

Come, you are a strange open man to tell everything thus.

CLERIMONT.

Why, believe it Dauphine, Truewit's a very honest fellow.

DAUPHINE.

I think no other, but this frank nature of his is not for secrets.

CLERIMONT.

Nay, then, you are mistaken, Dauphine. I know where he 5
has been well trusted, and discharg'd the trust very truly
and heartily.

DAUPHINE.

I contend not, Ned, but with the fewer a business is carried,
it is ever the safer. Now we are alone, if you'll go thither, I
am for you.   10

CLERIMONT.

When were you there?

DAUPHINE.

Last night, and such a *Decameron* of sport fallen out!
Boccace never thought of the like. Daw does nothing but
court her, and the wrong way. He would lie with her and
praises her modesty; desires that she would talk and be 15
free, and commends her silence in verses, which he reads
and swears are the best that ever man made. Then rails at
his fortunes, stamps, and mutines why he is not made a
counselor and call'd to affairs of state.

CLERIMONT.

I pray thee let's go. I would fain partake this. Some 20
water, boy.   [*Exit* Boy.]

DAUPHINE.

We are invited to dinner together, he and I, by one that
came thither to him, Sir La Foole.

1.] *preceded in F1 by S.D.*: Dauphine,
Clerimont, Boy.

---

18. *mutines*] speaks mutinously.
20–21. *Some water*] secure us a boat for travel up or down the river.

CLERIMONT.

Oh, that's a precious manikin!

DAUPHINE.

Do you know him?   25

CLERIMONT.

Ay, and he will know you too, if e'er he saw you but once,
though you should meet him at church in the midst of prayers. He is one of the Braveries though he be none o' the Wits.
He will salute a judge upon the bench and a bishop in the
pulpit, a lawyer when he is pleading at the bar, and a lady   30
when she is dancing in a masque, and put her out. He does
give plays and suppers, and invites his guests to 'em aloud,
out of his windore as they ride by in coaches. He has a
lodging in the Strand for the purpose, or to watch when
ladies are gone to the china-houses or the Exchange, that   35
he may meet 'em by chance and give 'em presents, some
two or three hundred pounds' worth of toys, to be laugh'd
at. He is never without a spare banquet or sweetmeats in his
chamber, for there women to alight at and come up to, for a
bait.   40

DAUPHINE.

Excellent! He was a fine youth last night, but now he is
much finer! What is his christen-name? I ha' forgot.

34. purpose, or] purpose. Or *F1*   39. for there] *F1* (*reset*); their *F1*
(*reset*); purpose: or *F1* (*orig.*).   (*orig.*).
36. presents] *F1* (*reset*); persents *F1*
(*orig.*).

24. *manikin*] "a little man, less than a man, to be played with like a
puppet" (Kittredge's comment on *Twelfth Night*, III.ii.57).
32. *give plays*] pays for private performances by the professional companies such as those at Blackfriars or Whitefriars.
34. *Strand*] the main street between Westminster and the City. Most of
the gentry lived in Drury Lane or on the Strand.
35. *china-houses*] stores selling oriental goods, a fashionable spot for
assignations (H.S.).
35. *the Exchange*] the seamster's and milliner's shops in Britain's Burse
on the Strand, opened 1609 (Sugden).
39–40. *for . . . bait*] so women may alight from their carriages and
come up to his chamber for a snack. The reading of F1, *their women*, seems
to refer back to "china-houses or the Exchange"; whereas *their* was a
spelling doublet of *there*.

[*Re-enter* Boy.]

CLERIMONT.

   Sir Amorous La Foole.

BOY.

   The gentleman is here below that owns that name.

CLERIMONT.

   'Heart, he's come to invite me to dinner, I hold my life.   45

DAUPHINE.

   Like enough. Pray thee, let's ha' him up.

CLERIMONT.

   Boy, marshall him.

BOY.

   With a truncheon, sir?

CLERIMONT.

   Away, I beseech you. [*Exit* Boy.]   I'll make him tell us
   his pedigree now, and what meat he has to dinner, and who   50
   are his guests, and the whole course of his fortuncs, with a
   breath.

[I.iv]   [*Enter*] La Foole.

LA FOOLE.

   'Save, dear Sir Dauphine, honor'd Master Clerimont.

CLERIMONT.

   Sir Amorous! You have very much honested my lodging
   with your presence.

LA FOOLE.

   Good faith, it is a fine lodging, almost as delicate a lodging
   as mine.   5

CLERIMONT.

   Not so, sir.

LA FOOLE.

   Excuse me, sir, if it were i' the Strand, I assure you. I am
   come, Master Clerimont, to entreat you wait upon two or
   three ladies to dinner today.

43. Sir] *F1* (*reset*); Sis *F1* (*orig.*).   [I.iv]
44. below] *F1* (*reset*); om. *F1* (*orig.*).   0.1.] La Foole, Clerimont, Dau-
44. owns] *F1* (*reset*); owes *F1* (*orig.*).   phine. *F1*.

   2. *honested*] honored.

CLERIMONT.

How, sir! Wait upon 'em? Did you ever see me carry   10
dishes?

LA FOOLE.

No, sir, dispense with me; I meant to bear 'em company.

CLERIMONT.

Oh, that I will, sir. The doubtfulness o' your phrase,
believe it, sir, would breed you a quarrel once an hour with
the terrible boys, if you should but keep 'em fellowship a day.   15

LA FOOLE.

It should be extremely against my will, sir, if I contested
with any man.

CLERIMONT.

I believe it, sir. Where hold you your feast?

LA FOOLE.

At Tom Otter's, sir.

DAUPHINE.

Tom Otter? What's he?   20

LA FOOLE.

Capatin Otter, sir. He is a kind of gamester, but he has had
command both by sea and by land.

DAUPHINE.

Oh, then he is *animal amphibium*?

LA FOOLE.

Ay sir. His wife was the rich china-woman that the courtiers
visited so often, that gave the rare entertainment. She   25
commands all at home.

CLERIMONT.

Then she is Captain Otter?

LA FOOLE.

You say very well, sir. She is my kinswoman, a La Foole
by the mother side, and will invite any great ladies for
my sake.   30

DAUPHINE.

Not of the La Fooles of Essex?

15. but] *F1 (reset)*; *om. F1 (orig.)*.

---

12. *dispense with*] excuse.
15. *terrible boys*] roisterers or roaring boys who fought private duels at
the least slight to their honor.

LA FOOLE.

No sir, the La Fooles of London.

CLERIMONT.

Now h'is in.

LA FOOLE.

They all come out of our house, the La Fooles o' the north,
the La Fooles of the west, the La Fooles of the east and   35
south—we are as ancient a family as any is in Europe—but
I myself am descended lineally of the French La Fooles—and
we do bear for our coat yellow or *or*, checker'd *azure* and
gules, and some three or four colors more, which is a very
noted coat and has sometimes been solemnly worn by   40
divers nobility of our house—but let that go, antiquity is not
respected now—I had a brace of fat does sent me, gentlemen,
and half a dozen of pheasants, a dozen or two of godwits,
and some other fowl, which I would have eaten while they
are good, and in good company—there will be a great lady   45
or two, my Lady Haughty, my Lady Centaur, Mistress Dol
Mavis—and they come a' purpose to see the silent gentlewoman, Mistress Epicoene, that honest Sir John Daw has
promis'd to bring thither—and then Mistress Trusty, my
Lady's woman, will be there too, and this honorable   50
knight, Sir Dauphine, with yourself, Master Clerimont—
and we'll be very merry and have fidlers and dance—I have
been a mad wag in my time and have spent some crowns
since I was a page in court to my Lord Lofty, and after my
Lady's gentleman-usher, who got me knighted in Ireland,   55
since it pleas'd my elder brother to die—I had as fair a gold
jerkin on that day as any was worn in the Island Voyage or
at Caliz, none disprais'd, and I came over in it hither,
show'd myself to my friends in court and after went down to

38. for] *F1 (reset)*; *om. F1 (orig.)*.

---

38. *coat*] coat of arms.

39. *gules*] red.

43. *godwits*] wading birds of the snipe family, a delicacy.

55. *knighted in Ireland*] The Earl of Essex cheapened knighthoods by
dubbing them in scores while on his Irish campaign.

57. *Island Voyage*] Essex's unsuccessful venture against the Azores, 1597.

58. *Caliz*] Cadiz, captured by the English fleet under Essex, 1596.
Ambitious gentlemen, such as John Donne, went on both these expeditions.

my tenants in the country and survey'd my lands, let new   60
leases, took their money, spent it in the eye o' the land
here, upon ladies—and now I can take up at my pleasure.

DAUPHINE.

Can you take up ladies, sir?

CLERIMONT.

Oh, let him breath, he has not recover'd.

DAUPHINE.

Would I were your half in that commodity—   65

LA FOOLE.

No sir, excuse me: I meant money, which can take up anything. I have another guest or two to invite and say as
much to, gentlemen. I'll take my leave abruptly, in hope you
will not fail—Your servant.   [*Exit* La Foole.]

DAUPHINE.

We will not fail you, sir precious La Foole; but she shall   70
that your ladies come to see, if I have credit afore Sir Daw.

CLERIMONT.

Did you ever hear such a wind-fucker as this?

DAUPHINE.

Or such a rook as the other, that will betray his mistress to
be seen! Come, 'tis time we prevented it.

CLERIMONT.

Go.   [*Exeunt.*]   75

[II.i]   [*Enter*] Morose, Mute.

MOROSE.

Cannot I yet find out a more compendious method than by
this trunk to save my servants the labor of speech and mine
ears the discord of sounds? Let me see: all discourses but
mine own afflict me, they seem harsh, impertinent, and
irksome. Is it not possible that thou should'st answer me by   5
signs, and I apprehend thee, fellow? Speak not, though I

---

65. commodity—] *F1 (reset)*; com-   66. S.P. LA FOOLE.] *F1 (reset)*; CLE.
modity. *F1 (orig.)*.   *F1 (orig.)*.

---

62. *take up*] borrow.
64. *breath*] i.e., take breath.
65. *were your half*] half as successful as you with the ladies (Bald).
72. *wind-fucker*] a kind of hawk.

question you. You have taken the ring off from the street
door as I bade you? Answer me not by speech but by silence,
unless it be otherwise. (*At the breaches, still the fellow makes legs
or signs.*) Very good. And you have fastened on a thick quilt   10
or flock-bed on the outside of the door, that if they knock
with their daggers or with brickbats, they can make no
noise? But with your leg, your answer, unless it be otherwise.
[Mute *makes a leg.*]   Very good. This is not only fit modesty
in a servant, but good state and discretion in a master. And   15
you have been with Cutbeard, the barber, to have him come
to me? [*Makes a leg.*] Good. And he will come presently?
Answer me not but with your leg, unless it be otherwise: if
it be otherwise, shake your head or shrug. [*Makes a leg.*] So.
Your Italian and Spaniard are wise in these, and it is a frugal   20
and comely gravity. How long will it be ere Cutbeard
come? Stay, if an hour, hold up your whole hand; if half an
hour, two fingers; if a quarter, one.   [Mute *holds up a
finger bent.*]   Good, half a quarter? 'Tis well. And have you
given him a key to come in without knocking? [*Makes*   25
a leg.] Good. And is the lock oil'd, and the hinges, today?
[*Makes a leg.*] Good. And the quilting of the stairs nowhere
worn out and bare? [*Makes a leg.*] Very good. I see by much
doctrine and impulsion it may be effected. Stand by. The
Turk in this divine discipline is admirable, exceeding all   30
the potentates of the earth; still waited on by mutes, and all
his commands so executed, yea, even in the war (as I have
heard) and in his marches, most of his charges and directions given by signs and with silence: an exquisite art! And
I am heartily asham'd and angry oftentimes that the princes   35
of Christendom should suffer a barbarian to transcend 'em
in so high a point of felicity. I will practice it hereafter.

One winds a horn without.

How now? Oh! Oh! What villain? What prodigy of man-
kind is that? Look.   [*Exit* Mute.] [*Horn sounds*] *again.*

9–10. S.D. (*At . . . signs*)] *marginal*   *within parentheses.*
note F1; from this point on in the scene,   22. your] *F1* (*reset*); you *F1* (*orig.*).
F1 designates Mute's business by a dash

---

9. *breaches*] interruptions, parentheses.
9. S.D. *makes legs*] bows.

Oh! Cut his throat, cut his throat: what murderer, hell- 40
hound, devil can this be?

[Re-enter Mute.]

MUTE.

It is a post from the court—

MOROSE.

Out rogue, and must thou blow thy horn too?

MUTE.

Alas, it is a post from the court, sir, that says he must
speak with you, pain of death—   45

MOROSE.

Pain of thy life, be silent.

[II.ii]

[Enter] Truewit [*booted and spurred, with a halter and post-horn in his hand.*]

TRUEWIT.

By your leave, sir (I am a stranger here), is your name Master
Morose? Is your name Master Morose? Fishes! Pythagoreans all! This is strange! What say you sir, nothing?
Has Harpocrates been here, with his club, among you?
Well sir, I will believe you to be the man at this time: I will 5
venture upon you, sir. Your friends at court commend 'em
to you, sir—

MOROSE [*aside*].

Oh men! Oh manners! Was there ever such an impudence?

TRUEWIT.

And are extremely solicitious for you, sir.

MOROSE.

Whose knave are you?   10

TRUEWIT.

Mine own knave and your compeer, sir.

MOROSE.

Fetch me my sword—

45. with] *F1 (reset)*; *om. F1 (orig.).*   *F1.*
[II.ii]   8. Oh ... impudence?]   (Oh ...
0.1.] Truewit, Morose, Cutbeard.   impudence?) *F1.*

2–3. *Pythagoreans*] silent.
4. *Harpocrates*] revenging son of Osiris, figured with a finger in his mouth.
"God of silence" (Cooper).

—25—

TRUEWIT.

    You shall taste the one half of my dagger if you do, groom, and you the other if you stir, sir. Be patient, I charge you in the king's name, and hear me without insurrection. They   15 say you are to marry? To marry! Do you mark, sir?

MOROSE.

    How then, rude companion!

TRUEWIT.

    Marry, your friends do wonder, sir, the Thames being so near, wherein you may drown so handsomely; or London Bridge at a low fall with a fine leap, to hurry you down the   20 stream; or such a delicate steeple i' the town as Bow, to vault from; or a braver height as Paul's; or if you affected to do it nearer home and a shorter way, an excellent garret windore into the street; or a beam in the said garret, with this halter (*he shows him a halter*), which they have sent, and desire   25 that you would sooner commit your grave head to this knot than to the wedlock noose; or take a little sublimate and go out of the world like a rat, or a fly (as one said) with a straw i' your arse: any way rather than to follow this goblin matrimony. Alas, sir, do you ever think to find a chaste wife in   30 these times? Now? When there are so many masques, plays, puritan preachings, mad folks, and other strange sights to be seen daily, private and public? If you had liv'd in King Ethelred's time, sir, or Edward the Confessor's, you might perhaps have found in some cold country hamlet, then, a   35 dull frosty wench would have been contented with one man: now, they will as soon be pleas'd with one leg or one eye. I'll tell you, sir, the monstrous hazards you shall run with a wife.

32. preachings] *F1* (*reset*); parleys
F1 (*orig.*).

---

    20. *low fall*] ebb tide, when water rushed through the narrow openings of the bridge.

    21. *Bow*] St. Mary-le-Bow church.

    27. *sublimate*] arsenic or mercuric chloride.

    28–29. *straw . . . arse*] in fly and spider fights, watched by coxcombs, a straw was thrust in the tail of a fly (H.S.).

    32. *preachings*] Jonson may have rejected *parleys* from the earlier setting of this forme to remove the association with the conference at Hampton Court (1604). *Preaching* figures prominently in Act III.

MOROSE.

Good sir! Have I ever cozen'd any friends of yours of their   40
land, bought their possessions, taken forfeit of their mortgage, begg'd a reversion from 'em, bastarded their issue?
What have I done that may deserve this?

TRUEWIT.

Nothing, sir, that I know, but your itch of marriage.

MOROSE.

Why, if I had made an assassinate upon your father,   45
vitiated your mother, ravished your sisters—

TRUEWIT.

I would kill you, sir, I would kill you if you had.

MOROSE.

Why, you do more in this, sir. It were a vengeance centuple
for all facinorous acts that could be nam'd, to do that you
do—   50

TRUEWIT.

Alas, sir, I am but a messenger: I but tell you what you
must hear. It seems your friends are careful after your soul's
health, sir, and would have you know the danger (but
you may do your pleasure for all them, I persuade not, sir).
If after you are married your wife do run away with a   55
vaulter, or the Frenchman that walks upon ropes, or him
that dances the jig, or a fencer for his skill at his weapon,
why it is not their fault; they have discharged their con-
sciences when you know what may happen. Nay, suffer
valiantly, sir, for I must tell you all the perils that you are   60
obnoxious to. If she be fair, young, and vegetous, no sweetmeats ever drew more flies; all the yellow doublets and
great roses i' the town will be there. If foul and crooked,
she'll be with them and buy those doublets and roses, sir.

61. to] *F3*; too *F1–2*.

---

42. *begg'd a reversion*] secured a right to succeed to an office.
42. *from*] away from.
46. *vitiated*] deflowered or violated (*OED*).
57. *weapon*] the first of several phallic insinuations in the play.
61. *obnoxious*] liable.
61. *vegetous*] lively.
63. *great roses*] shoe roses, ribbons gathered in a knot and fastened to
the instep, worn by gallants.

If rich and that you marry her dowry, not her, she'll reign in   65
your house as imperious as a widow. If noble, all her
kindred will be your tyrannes. If fruitful, as proud as May
and humorous as April; she must have her doctors, her mid-
wives, her nurses, her longings every hour, though it be for
the dearest morsel of man. If learned, there was never such   70
a parrot; all your patrimony will be too little for the
guests that must be invited to hear her speak Latin and
Greek, and you must lie with her in those languages too if
you will please her. If precise, you must feast all the
silenc'd brethren, once in three days; salute the sisters; en-   75
tertain the whole family or wood of 'em, and hear long-
winded exercises, singings, and catechizings, which you are
not given to and yet must give for, to please the zealous
matron your wife, who for the holy cause will cozen you over
and above. You begin to sweat, sir? But this is not half, i'   80
faith: you may do your pleasure notwithstanding, as I said
before, I come not to persuade you.

The Mute *is stealing away.*

Upon my faith, master servingman, if you do stir, I will
beat you.

MOROSE.

Oh, what is my sin! What is my sin?   85

TRUEWIT.

Then if you love your wife, or rather dote on her, sir, oh how
she'll torture you and take pleasure i' your torments! You
shall lie with her but when she lists; she will not hurt her
beauty, her complexion; or it must be for that jewel or that
pearl when she does; every half hour's pleasure must be   90
bought anew, and with the same pain and charge you woo'd
her at first. Then you must keep what servants she please,
what company she will; that friend must not visit you
without her license; and him she loves most she will seem to
hate eagerliest, to decline your jealousy; or feign to be   95

---

67. *tyrannes*] tyrants.   68. *humorous*] capricious.
74. *precise*] a puritan.
75. *silenc'd brethren*] puritan clergy who lost their licenses to preach after
the Hampton Court Conference.
76. *wood*] crowd.

jealous of you first, and for that cause go live with her she-
friend or cousin at the college, that can instruct her in all
the mysteries of writing letters, corrupting servants, taming
spies; where she must have that rich gown for such a great
day, a new one for the next, a richer for the third; be serv'd 100
in silver, have the chamber fill'd with a succession of grooms,
footmen, ushers, and other messengers, besides embroiderers, jewelers, tirewomen, sempsters, feathermen, per-
fumers; while she feels not how the land drops away, nor the
acres melt, nor foresees the change when the mercer has 105
your woods for her velvets; never weighs what her pride
costs, sir, so she may kiss a page or a smooth chin that has
the despair of a beard; be a stateswoman, know all the
news: what was done at Salisbury, what at the Bath, what
at court, what in progress; or so she may censure poets and 110
authors and styles, and compare 'em, Daniel with Spenser,
Jonson with the t'other youth, and so forth; or be thought
cunning in controversies or the very knots of divinity, and
have often in her mouth the state of the question, and then
skip to the mathematics and demonstration: and answer 115
in religion to one, in state to another, in bawdry to a third.

MOROSE.

Oh, oh!

TRUEWIT.

All this is very true, sir. And then her going in disguise to that
conjurer and this cunning woman, where the first question
is how soon you shall die; next, if her present servant love 120
her; next that, if she shall have a new servant, and how
many; which of her family would make the best bawd,
male or female; what precedence she shall have by her

115. demonstration:]   demonstration *F1*.

---

103. *tirewoman*] dressmakers.
103. *sempsters*] tailors.
110. *in progress*] the king's official visits around the provinces.
110. *censure*] judge.
112. *t'other youth*] possibly Dekker, or Marston.
114. *state of the question*] "*Estat* . . . the state, head, issue, knot, principal
point of a matter in controversy" (Cotgrave).
121. *servant*] lover.

next match? And sets down the answers, and believes 'em
above the scriptures. Nay, perhaps she'll study the art.   125

MOROSE.

Gentle sir, ha' you done? Ha' you had your pleasure o' me?
I'll think of these things.

TRUEWIT.

Yes, sir: and then comes reeking home of vapor and sweat
with going afoot, and lies in a month of a new face, all oil
and birdlime, and rinses in asses' milk, and is cleans'd with a 130
new fucus; God b'w'you, sir. One thing more (which I had
almost forgot). This too, with whom you are to marry, may
have made a conveyance of her virginity aforehand, as your
wise widows do of their states before they marry, in trust to
some friend, sir: who can tell? Or if she have not done it yet, 135
she may do, upon the wedding day or the night before, and
antedate you cuckold. The like has been heard of in nature.
'Tis no devis'd impossible thing, sir. God b'w'you: I'll be
bold to leave this rope with you, sir, for a remembrance.
Farewell, Mute.   [*Exit.*] 140

MOROSE.

Come, ha' me to my chamber, but first shut the door.

                                        The horn again.

Oh, shut the door, shut the door. Is he come again?

                    [*Enter* Cutbeard.]

CUTBEARD.

'Tis I, sir, your barber.

MOROSE.

Oh, Cutbeard, Cutbeard, Cutbeard, here has been a cut-
throat with me; help me in to my bed and give me physic 145
with thy counsel.   [*Exeunt.*]

130. rinses] *Cunningham*; rises *F1*.

---

130. *rinses*] although *rises* (see textual note) is an attractive reading
because of the contrast with *lies in, rinses* is probably what Jonson wrote.
Illo lacte fovetur propter quod secum commites educit ascellas: "She bathes herself
in that milk for which she takes a herd of asses in her train" (Juvenal,
Satires, VI, 469–470).

131. *fucus*] cosmetic.

[II.iii]   [*Enter*] Daw, Clerimont, Dauphine, Epicoene.

DAW.

Nay, and she will, let her refuse at her own charges; 'tis
nothing to me, gentlemen. But she will not be invited to the
like feasts or guests every day.

CLERIMONT.

Oh, by no means, she may not refuse—(*they dissuade her
privately*) to stay at home if you love your reputation.   5
'Slight, you are invited thither o' purpose to be seen and
laugh'd at by the lady of the college and her shadows. This
trumpeter hath proclaim'd you.

DAUPHINE.

You shall not go; let him be laugh'd at in your stead, for
not bringing you, and put him to his extemporal faculty of   10
fooling and talking loud to satisfy the company.

CLERIMONT.

He will suspect us, talk aloud. —Pray, Mistress Epicoene,
let's see your verses; we have Sir John Daw's leave; do not
conceal your servant's merit and your own glories.

EPICOENE.

They'll prove my servant's glories if you have his leave so   15
soon.

DAUPHINE.

His vainglories, lady!

DAW.

Shew 'em, shew 'em, mistress, I dare own 'em.

EPICOENE.

Judge you, what glories!

DAW.

Nay, I'll read 'em myself too; an author must recite his own   20
works. It is a madrigal of modesty.
            Modest and fair, for fair and good are near
                        Neighbors, howe're.—

DAUPHINE.

Very good.

CLERIMONT.

Ay, is't not?   25

---

1. *charges*] expense.

DAW.   *No noble virtue ever was alone,*
                              But two in one.

DAUPHINE.

Excellent!

CLERIMONT.

That again, I pray, Sir John.

DAUPHINE.

It has something in't like rare wit and sense.   30

CLERIMONT.

Peace.

DAW.   *No noble virtue ever was alone,*
                              But two in one.
                    Then, when I praise sweet modesty, I praise
                              Bright beauty's rays: 35
                    And having prais'd both beauty and modesty,
                              I have prais'd thee.

DAUPHINE.

Admirable!

CLERIMONT.

How it chimes and cries tink i' the close, divinely!

DAUPHINE.

Ay, 'tis Seneca.   40

CLERIMONT.

No, I think 'tis Plutarch.

DAW.

The dor on Plutarch and Seneca, I hate it: they are mine
own imaginations, by that light. I wonder those fellows
have such credit with gentlemen!

CLERIMONT.

They are very grave authors.   45

DAW.

Grave asses! Mere essayists! A few loose sentences and that's
all. A man would talk so his whole age; I do utter as good
things every hour, if they were collected and observ'd, as
either of 'em.

---

42. *The dor on*] to hell with (Bald).
46. *essayists*] such as Montaigne or Bacon; a bad pun on *asses*.

DAUPHINE.

  Indeed, Sir John!   50

CLERIMONT.

  He must needs, living among the Wits and Braveries too.

DAUPHINE.

  Ay, and being president of 'em as he is.

DAW.

  There's Aristotle, a mere commonplace fellow; Plato, a
  discourser; Thucidides and Livy, tedious and dry; Tacitus,
  an entire knot, sometimes worth the untying, very seldom.   55

CLERIMONT.

  What do you think of the poets, Sir John?

DAW.

  Not worthy to be nam'd for authors. Homer, an old tedious
  prolix ass, talks of curriers and chines of beef. Virgil, of
  dunging of land, and bees. Horace, of I know not what.

CLERIMONT.

  I think so.   60

DAW.

  And so Pindarus, Lycophron, Anacreon, Catullus, Seneca
  the tragedian, Lucan, Propertius, Tibullus, Martial,
  Juvenal, Ausonius, Statius, Politian, Valerius Flaccus, and
  the rest—

CLERIMONT.

  What a sack full of their names he has got!   65

DAUPHINE.

  And how he pours 'em out! Politian with Valerius Flaccus!

53. There's] *F1* (*corr.*); There is *F1*
(*uncorr.*).

---

  58. *chines of beef*] In *Iliad*, vii, 321, Agamemnon gave Ajax "the whole
length of the chine" of an ox (H.S.).

  59. *bees*] in his *Georgics*.

  61. *Lycophron*] "A Grammarian and writer of tragedies" (Cooper),
known for obscurity.

  65. *What . . . got!*] Presumably Daw hears all the following unflattering
remarks, but he is too stupid to perceive their irony.

  66. *Politian*] a brilliant Italian humanist (1454–1494).

  66. *Valerius Flaccus*] a dull Latin romancer, imitator of Apollonius of
Rhodes, in his *Argonautica*. Jonson objected to the sprawling disunity of such
tales.

CLERIMONT.

    Was not the character right of him?

DAUPHINE.

    As could be made, i' faith.

DAW.

    And Persius, a crabbed coxcomb not to be endur'd.

DAUPHINE.

    Why, whom do you account for authors, Sir John Daw?   70

DAW.

    Syntagma juris civilis, Corpus juris civilis, Corpus juris canonici,
the King of Spain's Bible.

DAUPHINE.

    Is the King of Spain's Bible an author?

CLERIMONT.

    Yes, and *Syntagma.*

DAUPHINE.

    What was that *Syntagma,* sir?   75

DAW.

    A civil lawyer, a Spaniard.

DAUPHINE.

    Sure, *Corpus* was a Dutchman.

CLERIMONT.

    Ay, both the *Corpusses,* I knew 'em: they were very cor-
pulent authors.

DAW.

    And then there's Vatablus, Pomponatius, Symancha; the 80
other are not to be receiv'd within the thought of a scholar.

DAUPHINE.

    'Fore God, you have a simple learn'd servant, lady, in
titles.

CLERIMONT.

    I wonder that he is not called to the helm and made a
counsellor!   85

---

    67. *character*] the portrait or character sketch given at I.ii.64 ff.
    71. *Syntagma . . . canonici*] *Syntagma* is the Greek equivalent of *corpus,*
hence the first two titles are essentially the same book, the standard collection of Roman law. The third is the corpus of canon law.
    80. *Vatablus . . . Symancha*] a sixteenth-century Hebrew scholar, a philos-
opher, and a jurist of minor repute.

DAUPHINE.

He is one extraordinary.

CLERIMONT.

Nay, but in ordinary! To say truth, the state wants such.

DAUPHINE.

Why, that will follow.

CLERIMONT.

I muse a mistress can be so silent to the dotes of such a
servant.   90

DAW.

'Tis her virtue, sir. I have written somewhat of her silence
too.

DAUPHINE.

In verse, Sir John?

CLERIMONT.

What else?

DAUPHINE.

Why, how can you justify your own being of a poet, that so   95
slight all the old poets?

DAW.

Why, every man that writes in verse is not a poet; you have
of the Wits that write verses and yet are no poets: they are
poets that live by it, the poor fellows that live by it.

DAUPHINE.

Why, would not you live by your verses, Sir John?   100

CLERIMONT.

No, 'twere pity he should. A knight live by his verses? He
did not make 'em to that end, I hope.

DAUPHINE.

And yet the noble Sidney lives by his, and the noble family
not asham'd.

CLERIMONT.

Ay, he profess'd himself; but Sir John Daw has more   105

---

89. *dotes*] endowments.

101. *live by his verses*] implying the stigma placed on a poet for selling his
works to a printer. Jonson was one of the first distinguished writers to defy
this convention, but he was the stepson of a bricklayer (son of a clergyman).

105. *profess'd*] openly admitted.

l.87: 'In ordinary' of officials: belonging to the regular staff –
probably here with a sense of special
duties (as in phys. in ordinary
to the Pr. of Wles.)

caution: he'll not hinder his own rising i' the state so much!
Do you think he will? Your verses, good Sir John, and no
poems.

DAW.   *Silence in woman is like speech in man,*
                            Deny't who can.   110

DAUPHINE.

Not I, believe it: your reason, sir.

DAW.   *Nor is't a tale*
                    That female vice should be a virtue male,
                    Or masculine vice, a female virtue be:
                            You shall it see   115 ◦
                            Prov'd with increase,
                    I know to speak and she to hold her peace.
Do you conceive me, gentlemen?

DAUPHINE.

No, faith, how mean you "with increase," Sir John?

DAW.

Why, with increase is when I court her for the common 120
cause of mankind, and she says nothing but *consentire videtur*,
and in time is *gravida*.

DAUPHINE.

Then this is a ballad of procreation?

CLERIMONT.

A madrigal of procreation, you mistake.

EPICOENE.

Pray give me my verses again, servant.   125

DAW.

If you'll ask 'em aloud, you shall.

                    [Epicoene *and* Daw *walk aside with the papers.*]

---

112. S.P. DAW.] *MS correc. F1   F1.*
(*DFo6*); DAV. *F1.*   126. you'll] *MS correc. F1 (DFo6)*;
124. procreation] *F2*; proceation   you you'll *F1.*

---

106. *hinder his own rising*] "They which once fall in the humor of versi-
fying, their heads are always full of as many crochets as new strooken
lovers ... and to men duely conversant in weighty and profitable affairs,
they are ... flat and tedious" (Sir John Melton, *A Six-folde Politician*, 1609,
sig. C8ᵛ).
    121. *consentire videtur*] seems to consent.
    122. *gravida*] pregnant.

CLERIMONT.

See, here's Truewit again!

[II.iv]   [*Enter*] Truewit [*with his post-horn*].

CLERIMONT.

Where hast thou been, in the name of madness, thus accout-
ered with thy horn?

TRUEWIT.

Where the sound of it might have pierc'd your senses with
gladness had you been in ear-reach of it. Dauphine, fall
down and worship me: I have forbid the bans, lad. I have   5
been with thy virtuous uncle and have broke the match.

DAUPHINE.

You ha' not, I hope.

TRUEWIT.

Yes, faith, and thou shouldst hope otherwise, I should repent me; this horn got me entrance, kiss it. I had no other
way to get in but by feigning to be a post; but when I got in   10
once, I prov'd none but rather the contrary, turn'd him into
a post or a stone or what is stiffer, with thund'ring into him
the incommodities of a wife and the miseries of marriage. If
ever Gorgon were seen in the shape of a woman, he hath seen
her in my description. I have put him off o' that scent forever.   15
Why do you not applaud and adore me, sirs? Why stand you
mute? Are you stupid? You are not worthy o' the benefit.

DAUPHINE.

Did not I tell you? mischief!—

CLERIMONT.

I would you had plac'd this benefit somewhere else.

TRUEWIT.

Why so?   20

CLERIMONT.

'Slight, you have done the most inconsiderate, rash, weak
thing that ever man did to his friend.

DAUPHINE.

Friend! If the most malicious enemy I have, had studied to
inflict an injury upon me, it could not be a greater.

0.1.] Clerimont, Truewit, Dauphine,
Cutbeard, Daw, Epicoene. *F1.*

---

10. *post*] messenger.

TRUEWIT.

Wherein, for God's sake? Gentlemen, come to yourselves   25
again.

DAUPHINE.

But I presag'd thus much afore to you.

CLERIMONT.

Would my lips had been solder'd when I spake on't. 'Slight,
what mov'd you to be thus impertinent?

TRUEWIT.

My masters, do not put on this strange face to pay my   30
courtesy: off with this visor. Have good turns done you and
thank 'em this way?

DAUPHINE.

'Fore heav'n, you have undone me. That which I have
plotted for and been maturing now these four months, you
have blasted in a minute; now I am lost, I may speak. This   35
gentlewoman was lodg'd here by me o' purpose, and to be
put upon my uncle, hath profess'd this obstinate silence for
my sake, being my entire friend, and one that for the requital
of such a fortune as to marry him, would have made me very
ample conditions: where now all my hopes are utterly   40
miscarried by this unlucky accident.

CLERIMONT.

Thus 'tis when a man will be ignorantly officious, do services
and not know his why; I wonder what courteous itch possess'd you! You never did absurder part i' your life nor a
greater trespass to friendship, to humanity.   45

DAUPHINE.

Faith, you may forgive it best: 'twas your cause principally.

CLERIMONT.

I know it, would it had not.

[*Enter* Cutbeard.]

DAUPHINE.

How now, Cutbeard, what news?

CUTBEARD.

The best, the happiest that ever was, sir. There has been

---

47. S.P. CLERIMONT.] *MS correc. F1*   48. S.P. DAUPHINE.] *MS correc. F1*
(*DFo6*); DLE. *F1*.   (*DFo6*); CAUP. *F1*.

44. *did*] played.

a mad gentleman with your uncle this morning (I think this   50
be the gentleman) that has almost talk'd him out of his wits
with threat'ning him from marriage—

DAUPHINE.

On, I pray thee.

CUTBEARD.

And your uncle, sir, he thinks 'twas done by your pro-
curement; therefore he will see the party you wot of,   55
presently, and if he like her, he says, and that she be so
inclining to dumb as I have told him, he swears he will
marry her today, instantly, and not defer it a minute longer.

DAUPHINE.

Excellent! Beyond our expectation!

TRUEWIT.

Beyond your expectation? By this light, I knew it would   60
be thus.

DAUPHINE.

Nay, sweet Truewit, forgive me.

TRUEWIT.

No, I was "ignorantly officious, impertinent"; this was the
"absurd, weak part."

CLERIMONT.

Wilt thou ascribe that to merit now, was mere fortune?   65

TRUEWIT.

Fortune? Mere providence. Fortune had not a finger in't.
I saw it must necessarily in nature f 'l out so; my genius is
never false to me in these things. Show me how it could
be otherwise.

DAUPHINE.

Nay, gentlemen, contend not, 'tis well now.   70

TRUEWIT.

Alas, I let him go on with "inconsiderate" and "rash" and
what he pleas'd.

CLERIMONT.

Away, thou strange justifier of thyself, to be wiser than
thou wert by the event.

---

56. *presently*] immediately.
74. *event*] outcome.

TRUEWIT.

Event! By this light, thou shalt never persuade me but I   75
foresaw it as well as the stars themselves.

DAUPHINE.

Nay, gentlemen, 'tis well now; do you two entertain Sir John
Daw with discourse while I send her away with instructions.

TRUEWIT.

I'll be acquainted with her first, by your favor.

[Epicoene *and* Daw *step forward.*]

CLERIMONT.

Master Truewit, lady, a friend of ours.   80

TRUEWIT.

I am sorry I have not known you sooner, lady, to celebrate
this rare virtue of your silence.

CLERIMONT.

'Faith, an' you had come sooner, you should ha' seen and
heard her well celebrated in Sir John Daw's madrigals.

TRUEWIT.

Jack Daw, God save you, when saw you La Foole?   85

[*Exeunt* Dauphine, Epicoene, Cutbeard.]

DAW.

Not since last night, Master Truewit.

TRUEWIT.

That's miracle! I thought you two had been inseparable.

DAW.

He's gone to invite his guests.

TRUEWIT.

Gods so, 'tis true! What a false memory have I towards that
man! I am one; I met him e'en now upon that he calls his   90
delicate fine black horse, rid into a foam with posting from
place to place and person to person to give 'em the cue—

CLERIMONT.

Lest they should forget?

TRUEWIT.

Yes, there was never poor captain took more pains at a
muster to show men than he at this meal to show friends.   95

---

91. *delicate*] exquisitely fine (*OED*).
95. *show men*] assemble recruits to verify the numbers.

l.93 C. speaks like a prompter!

DAW.

It is his quarter-feast, sir.

CLERIMONT.

What, do you say so, Sir John?

TRUEWIT.

Nay, Jack Daw will not be out, at the best friends he has,
to the talent of his wit: where's his mistress, to hear and
applaud him? Is she gone?   100

DAW.

Is Mistress Epicoene gone?

CLERIMONT.

Gone afore with Sir Dauphine, I warrant, to the place.

TRUEWIT.

Gone afore! That were a manifest injury, a disgrace and a
half, to refuse him at such a festival time as this, being a
Bravery and a Wit too.   105

CLERIMONT.

Tut, he'll swallow it like cream: he's better read in *jure
civili* than to esteem anything a disgrace is offer'd him
from a mistress.

DAW.

Nay, let her e'en go; she shall sit alone and be dumb in
her chamber a week together, for John Daw, I warrant her. 110
Does she refuse me?

CLERIMONT.

No, sir, do not take it so to heart. She does not refuse
you, but a little neglect you. Good faith, Truewit, you
were to blame to put it into his head that she does refuse
him.   115

TRUEWIT.

She does refuse him, sir, palpably, however you mince it.
An' I were as he, I would swear to speak ne'er a word to
her today for't.

DAW.

By this light, no more I will not.

TRUEWIT.

Nor to anybody else, sir.   120

'96. *quarter-feast*] given every quarter sessions when people flocked to
town.

3   −41−

DAW.

Nay, I will not say so, gentlemen.

CLERIMONT.

It had been an excellent happy condition for the company
if you could have drawn him to it.

DAW.

I'll be very melancholic, i' faith.

CLERIMONT.

As a dog, if I were as you, Sir John.   125

TRUEWIT.

Or a snail or a hog-louse: I would roll myself up for this
day, in troth, they should not unwind me.

DAW.

By this pick-tooth, so I will.

CLERIMONT.

'Tis well done; he begins already to be angry with his
teeth.   130

DAW.

Will you go, gentlemen?

CLERIMONT.

Nay, you must walk alone if you be right melancholic, Sir
John.

TRUEWIT.

Yes, sir, we'll dog you, we'll follow you afar off.   [*Exit* Daw.]

CLERIMONT.

Was there ever such a two yards of knighthood measur'd out 135
by time to be sold to laughter?

TRUEWIT.

A mere talking mole! Hang him, no mushroom was ever so
fresh. A fellow so utterly nothing, as he knows not what he
would be.

CLERIMONT.

Let's follow him, but first let's go to Dauphine; he's hovering 140
about the house to hear what news.

TRUEWIT.

Content.   [*Exeunt.*]

---

128. *pick-tooth*] toothpick.
137. *mole*] mola, a mooncalf or monstrous birth, an idiot (*OED*).
137. *mushroom*] "these mushrump gentlemen, That shoot up in a night"
(*Every Man Out of His Humor*, I.ii.162–163).

[II.v]   [*Enter*] Morose, Epicoene, Cutbeard, Mute.

MOROSE.

Welcome, Cutbeard; draw near with your fair charge,
and in her ear softly entreat her to unmask. [*She unmasks.*]
So. Is the door shut? [Mute *makes a leg.*] Enough. Now
Cutbeard, with the same discipline I use to my family, I
will question you. As I conceive, Cutbeard, this gentle-   5
woman is she you have provided and brought in hope she
will fit me in the place and person of a wife? Answer me
not but with your leg, unless it be otherwise. [*He makes a
leg.*] Very well done, Cutbeard. I conceive besides, Cutbeard, you have been pre-acquainted with her birth, edu-   10
cation, and qualities, or else you would not prefer her to my
acceptance, in the weighty consequence of marriage. [*Makes
a leg.*] This I conceive, Cutbeard. Answer me not but with
your leg, unless it be otherwise. [*Makes another leg.*] Very
well done, Cutbeard. Give aside now a little and leave me   15
to examine her condition and aptitude to my affection. (*He
goes about her and views her.*) She is exceeding fair and of a
special good favor; a sweet composition or harmony of limbs;
her temper of beauty has the true height of my blood. The
knave hath exceedingly well fitted me without. I will now try 20
her within. —Come near, fair gentlewoman; let not my
behavior seem rude, though unto you, being rare, it may
happly appear strange. (*She curtsies.*) Nay, lady, you may
speak, though Cutbeard and my man might not, for of all
sounds only the sweet voice of a fair lady has the just length 25
of mine ears. I beseech you, say, lady; out of the first fire of
meeting eyes (they say) love is stricken: do you feel any such
motion suddenly shot into you from any part you see in
me? Ha, lady? (*Curtsy.*) Alas lady, these answers by silent

---

1. your] *Q*; you *F1.*   *scene are designated by parentheses in F1.*
3. S.D.] *All bracketed S.D.s in this*   23. happly] happely *F1.*

---

11. *prefer*] offer.   18. *favor*] appearance.
18. *sweet*] well-tuned.
19. *temper*] delicate adjustment, as a musical instrument is tempered.
19. *height*] high pitch.
22. *rare*] inexperienced socially.
25–26. *just length of*] attuned to, as is a string of a viol.

curtsies from you are too courtless and simple. I have ever   30
had my breeding in court, and she that shall be my wife
must be accomplished with courtly and audacious orna-
ments. Can you speak, lady?

EPICOENE.

Judge you, forsooth.   *She speaks softly.*

MOROSE.

What say you, lady? Speak out, I beseech you.   35

EPICOENE.

Judge you, forsooth.

MOROSE.

O' my judgment, a divine softness! But can you naturally,
lady, as I enjoin these by doctrine and industry, refer yourself to the search of my judgment and (not taking pleasure
in your tongue, which is a woman's chiefest pleasure) think   40
it plausible to answer me by silent gestures, so long as my
speeches jump right with what you conceive? (*Curtsy.*)
Excellent! Divine! If it were possible she should hold out
thus! Peace, Cutbeard, thou art made forever as thou hast
made me, if this felicity have lasting; but I will try her   45
further. Dear lady, I am courtly, I tell you, and I must have
mine ears banqueted with pleasant and witty conferences,
pretty girds, scoffs, and daliance in her that I mean to choose
for my bed-phere. The ladies in court think it a most
desperate impair to their quickness of wit and good   50
carriage if they cannot give occasion for a man to court
'em, and when an amorous discourse is set on foot, minister
as good matter to continue it as himself, and do you alone
so much differ from all them that what they (with so much
circumstance) affect and toil for, to seem learn'd, to seem   55
judicious, to seem sharp and conceited, you can bury in
yourself with silence, and rather trust your graces to the
fair conscience of virtue than to the world's or your own
proclamation?

---

30. *courtless*] uncourtly (this passage the only example in *OED*).
38. *industry*] practice.   42. *jump right with*] tally with (*OED*).
48. *girds*] taunts.   49. *bed-phere*] bedfellow (*OED*).
55. *circumstance*] formality.   56. *conceited*] ingenious, imaginative.
58. *conscience*] consciousness.

EPICOENE.

I should be sorry else. 60

MOROSE.

What say you, lady? Good lady, speak out.

EPICOENE.

I should be sorry, else.

MOROSE.

That sorrow doth fill me with gladness! Oh, Morose, thou
art happy above mankind! Pray that thou mayest contain
thyself. I will only put her to it once more, and it shall be 65
with the utmost touch and test of their sex. But hear me, fair
lady, I do also love to see her whom I shall choose for my
heicfar to be the first and principal in all fashions, precede
all the dames at court by a fortnight, have her council of
tailors, lineners, lace-women, embroiderers, and sit with 70
'em sometimes twice a day upon French intelligences, and
then come forth varied like Nature, or oft'ner than she, and
better by the help of Art, her emulous servant. This do I
affect. And how will you be able, lady, with this frugality
of speech, to give the manifold (but necessary) instruc- 75
tions for that bodice, these sleeves, those skirts, this cut, that
stitch, this embroidery, that lace, this wire, those knots, that
ruff, those roses, this girdle, that fan, the t'other scarf, these
gloves? Ha, what say you, lady?

EPICOENE.

I'll leave it to you, sir. 80

MOROSE.

How lady? Pray you, rise a note.

EPICOENE.

I leave it to wisdom and you, sir.

MOROSE.

Admirable creature! I will trouble you no more; I will not
sin against so sweet a simplicity. Let me now be bold to print

76. bodice] bodies *F1*.

---

68. *heicfar*] heifer, wife. "If you had not plowed with my heifer..."
Judges, 14:18 (H.S.).

71. *intelligences*] news.

76. *bodice*] a complicated two-part covering over the top of a smock,
like a corset, stiffened with whalebone, that kept the belly flat (Camden).

on those divine lips the seal of being mine. Cutbeard, I give   85
thee the lease of thy house free; thank me not, but with
thy leg. [*Makes a leg.*] I know what thou wouldst say, she's
poor and her friends deceased; she has brought a wealthy
dowry in her silence, Cutbeard, and in respect of her poverty,
Cutbeard, I shall have her more loving and obedient,   90
Cutbeard. Go thy ways and get me a minister presently,
with a soft, low voice, to marry us, and pray him he will not
be impertinent, but brief as he can; away; softly, Cutbeard.
                                        [*Exit* Cutbeard.]
Sirrah, conduct your mistress into the dining room, your
now-mistress.   [*Exeunt* Mute *and* Epicoene.]   95
Oh my felicity! How I shall be reveng'd on mine insolent
kinsman and his plots to fright me from marrying! This night
I will get an heir and thrust him out of my blood like a
stranger; he would be knighted, forsooth, and thought by
that means to reign over me, his title must do it: no, kins-   100
man, I will now make you bring me the tenth lord's and the
sixteenth lady's letter, kinsman, and it shall do you no good,
kinsman. Your knighthood itself shall come on its knees, and
it shall be rejected; it shall be sued for its fees to execution
and not be redeem'd; it shall cheat at the twelvepenny   105
ordinary, it knighthood, for its diet all the term time, and
tell tales for it in the vacation to the hostess; or it knighthood shall do worse; take sanctuary in Coleharbour, and
fast. It shall fright all it friends with borrowing letters, and
when one of the forescore hath brought it knighthood ten   110
shillings, it knighthood shall go to the Cranes or the Bear at

---

93. *impertinent*] irrelevant.
104. *fees to execution*] sued right up to the time when the writ of seizure
is served (Bald).
105–106. *twelvepenny ordinary*] an inferior place to eat; a two shilling meal
was better.
106. *it*] archaic form of *its, his.*
107. *tell tales*] the hostess at a restaurant would give free meals to someone
who could spark the table conversations.
108. *Coleharbour*] Cold Harbour, sanctuary for debtors, where they were
free from arrest.
111. *Cranes*] the Three Cranes in the Vintry, haunt of pretenders to wit.
111–112. *Bear at the Bridge-foot*] a popular tavern on the Surrey side of
the river.

the Bridge-foot and be drunk in fear; it shall not have money
to discharge one tavern reckoning, to invite the old creditors
to forbear it knighthood, or the new that should be, to trust
it knighthood. It shall be the tenth name in the bond, to   115
take up the commodity of pipkins and stone jugs, and the part
thereof shall not furnish it knighthood forth for the attempt-
ing of a baker's widow, a brown baker's widow. It shall give it
knighthood's name for a stallion to all gamesome citizens'
wives and be refus'd, when the master of a dancing school   120
or (how do you call him?) the worst reveler in the town is
taken; it shall want clothes, and by reason of that, wit to fool
to lawyers. It shall not have hope to repair itself by Constan-
tinople, Ireland, or Virginia; but the best and last fortune
to it knighthood shall be to make Dol Tear-sheet or Kate   125
Common a lady, and so it knighthood may eat.   [*Exit.*]

[II.vi]   [*Enter*] Truewit, Dauphine, Clerimont.

TRUEWIT.
   Are you sure he is not gone by?
DAUPHINE.
   No, I stayed in the shop ever since.
CLERIMONT.
   But he may take the other end of the lane.
DAUPHINE.
   No, I told him I would be here at this end; I appointed him
   hither.   5
TRUEWIT.
   What a barbarian it is to stay then!

                  [*Enter* Cutbeard.]
DAUPHINE.
   Yonder he comes.

0.1.] Truewit, Dauphine, Clerimont, Cutbeard. *F1.*

---

115. *tenth name*] tenth man to be paid off, if there should ever be any
"commodity" or profit to be made on the resale of goods. Money lenders
forced a borrower to take part of his loan in worthless items.
   124. *Virginia*] "I'll to Virginia like some cheating bankrupt, and leave
my creditor in the suds," S. S., *The Honest Lawyer*, 1616 (H.S.).
   125. *Dol Tear-sheet*] the foul-mouthed whore of Shakespeare's *2 Henry IV*.

CLERIMONT.

> And his charge left behind him, which is a very good sign,
> Dauphine.

DAUPHINE.

> How now, Cutbeard, succeeds it or no?   10

CUTBEARD.

> Past imagination, sir, *omnia secunda*; you could not have
> pray'd to have had it so well: *Saltat senex*, as it is i' the
> proverb, he does triumph in his felicity; admires the party!
> He has given me the lease of my house too! And I am now
> going for a silent minister to marry 'em, and away.   15

TRUEWIT.

> 'Slight, get one o' the silenc'd ministers, a zealous brother
> would torment him purely.

CUTBEARD.

> *Cum privilegio*, sir.

DAUPHINE.

> Oh, by no means, let's do nothing to hinder it now; when
> 'tis done and finished, I am for you, for any device of   20
> vexation.

CUTBEARD.

> And that shall be within this half hour, upon my dexterity,
> gentlemen. Contrive what you can in the meantime, *bonis
> avibus*.   [*Exit.*]

CLERIMONT.

> How the slave doth Latin it!   25

TRUEWIT.

> It would be made a jest to posterity, sirs, this day's mirth,
> if ye will.

CLERIMONT.

> Beshrew his heart that will not, I pronounce.

---

11. *omnia secunda*] everything favorable.
12. *Saltat senex*] the old boy is cutting capers (H.S.).
17. *purely*] completely.
18. *Cum privilegio*] with authority, a formula used in the license to print a book.
23–24. *bonis avibus*] the omens being favorable.
25. *Latin*] since barbers doubled as surgeons, they were likely to affect learned languages. A barber in Jonson's *The Staple of News* also speaks Latin.

DAUPHINE.

And for my part. What is't?

TRUEWIT.

To translate all La Foole's company and his feast hither   30
today, to celebrate this bride-ale.

DAUPHINE.

Ay, marry, but how will't be done?

TRUEWIT.

I'll undertake the directing of all the lady guests thither,
and then the meat must follow.

CLERIMONT.

For God's sake, let's effect it; it will be an excellent comedy   35
of affliction, so many several noises.

DAUPHINE.

But are they not at the other place already, think you?

TRUEWIT.

I'll warrant you for the college-honors: one o' their faces
has not the priming color laid on yet, nor the other her
smock sleek'd.   40

CLERIMONT.

Oh, but they'll rise earlier than ordinary to a feast.

TRUEWIT.

Best go see and assure ourselves.

CLERIMONT.

Who knows the house?

TRUEWIT.

I'll lead you. Were you never there yet?

DAUPHINE.

Not I.   45

CLERIMONT.

Nor I.

TRUEWIT.

Where ha' you liv'd then? Not know Tom Otter!

CLERIMONT.

No. For God's sake, what is he?

---

30. *translate*] transfer.
31. *bride-ale*] wedding feast.
40. *sleek'd*] ironed.

TRUEWIT.

An excellent animal, equal with your Daw or La Foole, if not
transcendent, and does Latin it as much as your barber;   50
he is his wife's subject; he calls her princess, and at such
times as these, follows her up and down the house like a
page, with his hat off, partly for heat, partly for reverence.
At this instant, he is marshaling of his bull, bear, and
horse.   55

DAUPHINE.

What be those, in the name of Sphinx?

TRUEWIT.

Why, sir, he has been a great man at the Bear Garden in his
time, and from that subtle sport has ta'en the witty de-
nomination of his chief carousing cups. One he calls his
bull, another his bear, another his horse. And then he has his 60
lesser glasses that he calls his deer and his ape, and several
degrees of 'em too, and never is well nor thinks any entertainment perfect, till these be brought out and set o' the
cupboard.

CLERIMONT.

For God's love! We should miss this if we should not go.   65

TRUEWIT.

Nay, he has a thousand things as good that will speak him
all day. He will rail on his wife with certain common-
places behind her back, and to her face—

DAUPHINE.

No more of him. Let's go see him, I petition you.   [*Exeunt.*]

---

50. *Latin it*] appropriate for Otter because a bearward put on an appearance of "great wisdom and gravity" and performed a parody of learned
dispute, according to *Robert Laneham's Letter* describing bearbaiting before
the Queen (ed. Furnivall, 1890, p. 16).

57. *Bear Garden*] or Paris Garden on the Bankside, an arena where bear-
baitings were held.

59–60. *his bull*] Drinking games using witty denominations from branches
of learning are described in the *Eighth Liberal Science*, 1650 (see Eric Partridge,
Dictionary of Slang, 1961, Vol. II supplement, s.v. *tavern*).

66. *speak*] reveal.

[III.i]

[*Enter*] Otter, Mistress Otter; Truewit, Clerimont, Dauphine
[*presently follow, unobserved*].

OTTER.

Nay good princess, hear me *pauca verba*.

MRS. OTTER.

By that light, I'll ha' you chain'd up with your bull-dogs
and bear-dogs, if you be not civil the sooner. I'll send you
to kennel, i' faith. You were best bait me with your bull, bear,
and horse! Never a time that the courtiers or collegiates   5
come to the house, but you make it a Shrove Tuesday! I
would have you get your Whitsuntide-velvet-cap and your
staff i' your hand to entertain 'em; yes in troth, do.

OTTER.

Not so, princess, neither, but under correction, sweet princess, gi' me leave—these things I am known to the courtiers   10
by. It is reported to them for my humor, and they receive
it so, and do expect it. Tom Otter's bull, bear, and horse
is known all over England, *in rerum natura*.

MRS. OTTER.

Fore me, I will *na-ture* 'em over to Paris Garden and *na-ture*
you thither too, if you pronounce 'em again. Is a bear a fit   15
beast, or a bull, to mix in society with great ladies? think i'
your discretion, in any good polity?

OTTER.

The horse then, good princess.

MRS. OTTER.

Well, I am contented for the horse; they love to be well
hors'd, I know. I love it myself.   20

OTTER.

And it is a delicate fine horse this. *Poetarum Pegasus.* Under

---

1. *pauca verba*] part of a proverb: "Few words show men wise" (Tilley,
W 799).
9. *under correction*] "subject to correction; a formula expressing deference
to superior information or critical authority" (*OED*).
11. *humor*] temperament, oddity of personality. Jonson would say Otter's
was an affection of a humor. See the induction to *Every Man Out of His
Humor*.
13. *in rerum natura*] in the world.   17. *polity*] society.
21. *Poetarum Pegasus*] the Pegasus of poets.

correction, princess, Jupiter did turn himself into a—*taurus*
or bull, under correction, good princess.

MRS. OTTER.

By my integrity, I'll send you over to the Bankside, I'll
commit you to the Master of the Garden, if I hear but a   25
syllable more. Must my house or my roof be polluted with
the scent of bears and bulls when it is perfum'd for great
ladies? Is this according to the instrument, when I married
you? That I would be princess and reign in mine own
house, and you would be my subject and obey me? What   30
did you bring me, should make you thus peremptory?
Do I allow you your half-crown a day to spend where you
will among your gamesters, to vex and torment me at such
times as these? Who gives you your maintenance, I pray
you? Who allows you your horsemeat and man's meat?   35
Your three suits of apparel a year? Your four pair of
stockings, one silk, three worsted? Your clean linen, your
bands, and cuffs when I can get you to wear 'em? 'Tis mar'l
you ha' 'em on now. Who graces you with courtiers or great
personages to speak to you out of their coaches and come   40
home to your house? Were you ever so much as look'd upon
by a lord or a lady before I married you, but on the Easter or
Whitsun-holidays, and then out at the Banqueting-House
windore, when Ned Whiting or George Stone were at the
stake?   45

TRUEWIT [*aside*].

For God's sake let's go stave her off him.

MRS. OTTER.

Answer me to that. And did not I take you up from thence

23.] *Gifford follows this line with S.D.:*   Dauphine *behind.*
Enter Truewit, Clerimont, *and*   46. For...him.] (For...him.) *F1.*

---

28. *instrument*] marriage agreement, a formal legal document.
35. *horsemeat*] horse fodder.
36. *three suits*] a servant's allowance (H.S.).
38. *mar'l*] marvel.
43. *Banqueting-House*] at the palace in Whitehall, where James I saw
bears and bulls from Southwark baited at Easter and Shrovetide.
44. *Whiting...Stone*] champion bears. George Stone died at court,
being baited before the King of Denmark in 1606 (H.S.).

in an old greasy buff-doublet with points and green velvet
sleeves out at the elbows? You forget this.

TRUEWIT [*aside*].

She'll worry him if we help not in time.   50

MRS. OTTER.

Oh, here are some o' the gallants! Go to, behave yourself
distinctly and with good morality, or I protest, I'll take
away your exhibition.

[III.ii]   Truewit, Clerimont, Dauphine [*come forward*].

TRUEWIT.

By your leave, fair Mistress Otter, I'll be bold to enter these
gentlemen in your acquaintance.

MRS. OTTER.

It shall not be obnoxious or difficil, sir.

TRUEWIT.

How does my noble Captain? Is the bull, bear, and horse
in *rerum natura* still?   5

OTTER.

Sir, *sic visum superis*.

MRS. OTTER.

I would you would but intimate 'em, do. Go your ways in,
and get toasts and butter made for the woodcocks. That's a
fit province for you.   [*Exit* Otter.]

CLERIMONT.

Alas, what a tyranny is this poor fellow married to.   10

TRUEWIT.

Oh, but the sport will be anon, when we get him loose.

DAUPHINE.

Dares he ever speak?

50. She'll . . . time.]   (She'll . . .   0.1.] Truewit, Mrs. Otter, Cap.
time.) *F1*.   Otter, Clerimont, Dauphine, Cut-
                                          beard. *F1*.

48. *points*] laces.   50. *worry*] as in bear-baiting.
52. *distinctly*] handsomely, "orderly" (Cotgrave).
53. *exhibition*] allowance.
[III.ii]
  6. *sic visum superis*] Thus it has seemed good to those above.
  7. *intimate*] "make yourself intimate with them"; an affected way of
saying "Go and join them."

TRUEWIT.

No Anabaptist ever rail'd with the like license: but mark her language in the meantime, I beseech you.

MRS. OTTER.

Gentlemen, you are very aptly come. My cousin, Sir   15
Amorous, will be here briefly.

TRUEWIT.

In good time, lady. Was not Sir John Daw here to ask for him and the company?

MRS. OTTER.

I cannot assure you, Master Truewit. Here was a very melancholy knight in a ruff, that demanded my subject for   20
somebody, a gentleman I think.

CLERIMONT.

Ay, that was he, lady.

MRS. OTTER.

But he departed straight, I can resolve you.

DAUPHINE.

What an excellent choice phrase this lady expresses in!

TRUEWIT.

Oh, sir, she is the only authentical courtier, that is not   25
naturally bred one, in the city.

MRS. OTTER.

You have taken that report upon trust, gentlemen.

TRUEWIT.

No, I assure you, the court governs it so, lady, in your behalf.

MRS. OTTER.

I am the servant of the court and courtiers, sir.   30

TRUEWIT.

They are rather your idolaters.

MRS. OTTER.

Not so, sir.

[*Enter* Cutbeard.]

---

13. *Anabaptist*] here, a puritan.
20. *subject*] i.e., Otter.
23. *resolve*] assure. Mrs. Otter has picked up a fashionable word from casuistry.
28. *governs*] determines.

DAUPHINE.

How now, Cutbeard? Any cross?

CUTBEARD.

Oh no, sir: *omnia bene*. 'Twas never better o' the hinges,
all's sure. I have so pleas'd him with a curate that he's gone   35
to't almost with the delight he hopes for soon.

DAUPHINE.

What is he, for a vicar?

CUTBEARD.

One that has catch'd a cold, sir, and can scarce be heard
six inches off, as if he spoke out of a bulrush that were not
pick'd, or his throat were full of pith: a fine quick fellow   40
and an excellent barber of prayers. I came to tell you, sir,
that you might *omnem movere lapidem* (as they say) be ready
with your vexation.

DAUPHINE.

Gramercy, honest Cutbeard, be thereabouts with thy key
to let us in.   45

CUTBEARD.

I will not fail you, sir: *ad manum*.   [*Exit.*]

TRUEWIT.

Well, I'll go watch my coaches.

DAUPHINE.

Do, and we'll send Daw to you if you meet him not.

[*Exit* Truewit.]

MRS. OTTER.

Is Master Truewit gone?

DAUPHINE.

Yes, lady, there is some unfortunate business fallen out.   50

MRS. OTTER.

So I judg'd by the physiognomy of the fellow that came in,
and I had a dream last night too of the new pageant and

---

34. *omnia bene*] all's well.

34. *o' the hinges*] never swung more easily (Bald).

39. *out of a bulrush*] a "bumping" or "mugient" noise, as of a bittern
whooping in a reed (Thomas Browne, *Vulgar Errors*, III.xxvii.4).

42. *omnem movere lapidem*] "leave no stone unturned"; a proverb from
Erasmus' *Adagia* (Tilley, S 890).

46. *ad manum*] at hand.

52. *pageant*] procession at the installation of a new Lord Mayor (Bald).

my Lady Mayoress, which is always very ominous to me.
I told it my Lady Haughty t'other day, when her honor
came hither to see some China stuffs, and she expounded   55
it out of Artemidorus, and I have found it since very true. It
has done me many affronts.

CLERIMONT.

Your dream, lady?

MRS. OTTER.

Yes, sir, anything I do but dream o' the city. It stain'd me
a damask tablecloth, cost me eighteen pound at one time;   60
and burnt me a black satin gown, as I stood by the fire at my
Lady Centaur's chamber in the college another time. A
third time, at the lord's masque, it dropp'd all my wire and
my ruff with wax candle, that I could not go up to the
banquet. A fourth time, as I was taking coach to go to Ware   65
to meet a friend, it dash'd me a new suit all over (a crimson
satin doublet and black velvet skirts) with a brewer's horse,
that I was fain to go in and shift me, and kept my chamber a
leash of days for the anguish of it.

DAUPHINE.

These were dire mischances, lady.   70

CLERIMONT.

I would not dwell in the city, and 'twere so fatal to me.

MRS. OTTER.

Yes, sir, but I do take advice of my doctor to dream of it as
little as I can.

DAUPHINE.

You do well, Mistress Otter.

[*Enter* Sir John Daw, *who is taken aside by* Clerimont.]

MRS. OTTER.

Will it please you to enter the house farther, gentlemen?   75

---

56. *Artemidorus*] Greek writer who believed dreams foretell the future.
63. *wire*] see Prologue, l. 23, note.
65. *Ware*] a place of assignations twenty miles north of London. See
V.i.57, note.
66–67. *crimson satin doublet*] The close fitting jacket was usually masculine attire, and red was reserved for royalty and the better classes.
68. *shift*] change.
68–69. *a leash of*] three.

DAUPHINE.

And your favor, lady; but we stay to speak with a knight,
Sir John Daw, who is here come. We shall follow you, lady.

MRS. OTTER.

At your own time, sir. It is my cousin Sir Amorous his
feast—

DAUPHINE.

I know it lady.   80

MRS. OTTER.

And mine together. But it is for his honor, and therefore I
take no name of it, more than of the place.

DAUPHINE.

You are a bounteous kinswoman.

MRS. OTTER.

Your servant, sir.   [*Exit.*]

[III.iii]

CLERIMONT [*coming forward with* Daw].

Why, do not you know it, Sir John Daw?

DAW.

No, I am a rook if I do.

CLERIMONT.

I'll tell you then, she's married by this time! And whereas
you were put i' the head that she was gone with Sir Dauphine, I assure you, Sir Dauphine has been the noblest,   5
honestest friend to you that ever gentleman of your quality
could boast of. He has discover'd the whole plot, and made
your mistress so acknowledging and indeed so ashamed of
her injury to you that she desires you to forgive her and but
grace her wedding with your presence today. She is to be   10
married to a very good fortune, she says, his uncle, old
Morose, and she will'd me in private to tell you that she
shall be able to do you more favors, and with more security
now, than before.

DAW.

Did she say so, i' faith?   15

1.] *preceded in F1 by S.D.:* Cleri-   Otter.
mont, Daw, La Foole, Dauphine,   1. Why,] *F3*; Why *F1*.

CLERIMONT.

 Why, what do you think of me, Sir John! Ask Sir Dauphine.

DAW.

 Nay, I believe you. Good Sir Dauphine, did she desire me to forgive her?

DAUPHINE.

 I assure you, Sir John, she did.

DAW.

 Nay, then, I do with all my heart, and I'll be jovial. 20

CLERIMONT.

 Yes, for look you sir, this was the injury to you. La Foole intended this feast to honor her bridal day, and made you the property to invite the college ladies and promise to bring her; and then at the time she should have appear'd (as his friend) to have given you the dor. Whereas now, Sir 25 Dauphine has brought her to a feeling of it, with this kind of satisfaction, that you shall bring all the ladies to the place where she is and be very jovial; and there she will have a dinner which shall be in your name, and so disappoint La Foole, to make you good again and (as it were) a saver i' 30 the main.

DAW.

 As I am a knight, I honor her and forgive her heartily.

CLERIMONT.

 About it then presently. Truewit is gone before to confront the coaches and to acquaint you with so much if he meet you. Join with him and 'tis well. 35

[Enter La Foole.]

 See, here comes your antagonist, but take you no notice, but be very jovial.

17. S.P. DAW.] *MS correc. F1 (DFo6)*, 31. main] *Whalley;* man *F1. Whalley;* DAVP. *F1.*

---

 23. *property*] tool.

 25. *given . . . dor*] disgraced you in the courtly competition between rivals for the hand of a mistress; elaborately explained in Jonson's *Cynthia's Revels,* V.ii.

 30. *saver*] one who escaped loss in the dice game of hazard. The main (like seven in craps) is determined before the game starts. Although as thrower you may lose heavily on your point (the chance), when someone else throws, you recoup your losses, if he shoots the main (Charles Cotton, *The Compleat Gamester,* 1674, Chapter XXXIV).

– 58 –

LA FOOLE.

Are the ladies come, Sir John Daw, and your mistress? Sir
Dauphine, you are exceeding welcome, and honest Master
Clerimont. Where's my cousin? Did you see no collegiates,   40
gentlemen?   [*Exit* Daw.]

DAUPHINE.

Collegiates! Do you not hear, Sir Amorous, how you are
abus'd?

LA FOOLE.

How, sir!

CLERIMONT.

Will you speak so kindly to Sir John Daw, that has done   45
you such an affront?

LA FOOLE.

Wherein, gentlemen? Let me be a suitor to you to know, I
beseech you!

CLERIMONT.

Why, sir, his mistress is married today to Sir Dauphine's
uncle, your cousin's neighbor, and he has diverted all the   50
ladies and all your company thither, to frustrate your provision and stick a disgrace upon you. He was here now to
have intic'd us away from you too, but we told him his own,
I think.

LA FOOLE.

Has Sir John Daw wrong'd me so inhumanly?   55

DAUPHINE.

He has done it, Sir Amorous, most maliciously and treacher-
ously; but if you'll be rul'd by us, you shall quit him, i'
faith.

LA FOOLE.

Good gentlemen! I'll make one, believe it. How, I pray?

DAUPHINE.

Marry, sir, get me your pheasants and your godwits and   60
your best meat, and dish it in silver dishes of your cousin's
presently, and say nothing, but clap me a clean towel about

51–52. *provision*] preparations.
57. *quit*] repay.
59. *make one*] join the group, play along with you.
60. *godwits*] see I.iv.43 note.

you like a sewer, and bare-headed march afore it with a
good confidence ('tis but over the way, hard by) and we'll
second you, where you shall set it o' the board, and bid 'em   65
welcome to't, which shall show 'tis yours and disgrace his
preparation utterly; and for your cousin, whereas she should
be troubled here at home with care of making and giving
welcome, she shall transfer all that labor thither and be a
principal guest herself, sit rank'd with the college-honors,   70
and be honor'd and have her health drunk as often, as bare,
and as loud as the best of 'em.

LA FOOLE.

I'll go tell her presently. It shall be done, that's resolv'd.

[*Exit.*]

CLERIMONT.

I thought he would not hear it out, but 'twould take him.

DAUPHINE.

Well, there be guests and meat now; how shall we do for   75
music?

CLERIMONT.

The smell of the venison going through the street will
invite one noise of fiddlers or other.

DAUPHINE.

I would it would call the trumpeters thither.

CLERIMONT.

Faith, there is hope; they have intelligence of all feasts.   80
There's good correspondence betwixt them and the London
cooks. 'Tis twenty to one but we have 'em.

DAUPHINE.

'Twill be a most solemn day for my uncle, and an excellent
fit of mirth for us.

CLERIMONT.

Ay, if we can hold up the emulation betwixt Foole and   85
Daw, and never bring them to expostulate.

---

63. *sewer*] a position of rank in a noble or royal household, in charge of
serving food.
71. *bare*] bareheaded, when a person's health is drunk.
78. *noise*] band.
85. *emulation*] ambitious rivalry.
86. *expostulate*] explain.

DAUPHINE.

Tut, flatter 'em both (as Truewit says) and you may take their understandings in a purse-net. They'll believe themselves to be just such men as we make 'em, neither more nor less. They have nothing, not the use of their senses, but by tradition. 90

[La Foole] *enters like a sewer.*

CLERIMONT.

See! Sir Amorous has his towel on already. Have you persuaded your cousin?

LA FOOLE.

Yes, 'tis very feasible; she'll do anything, she says, rather than the La Fooles shall be disgrac'd. 95

DAUPHINE.

She is a noble kinswoman. It will be such a pestling device, Sir Amorous! It will pound all your enemy's practices to powder and blow him up with his own mine, his own train.

LA FOOLE.

Nay, we'll give fire, I warrant you.

CLERIMONT.

But you must carry it privately, without any noise, and take 100 no notice by any means—

[*Enter* Otter.]

OTTER.

Gentlemen, my princess says you shall have all her silver dishes, *festinate*; and she's gone to alter her tire a little and go with you—

CLERIMONT.

And yourself too, Captain Otter. 105

DAUPHINE.

By any means, sir.

---

88. *purse-net*] a bag-shaped net, used for catching rabbits (*OED*).

96. *pestling*] crushing, like a pestle.

98. *train*] lure, a tricky device. The opposition between La Foole and Daw is spoken of increasingly in terms of clichés of revenge tragedy, with plot and counterplot, antagonists, and mines.

100. *carry*] manage.

103. *festinate*] quickly.

OTTER.

Yes, sir, I do mean it; but I would entreat my cousin Sir
Amorous and you gentlemen to be suitors to my princess,
that I may carry my bull and my bear, as well as my horse.

CLERIMONT.

That you shall do, Captain Otter.   110

LA FOOLE.

My cousin will never consent, gentlemen.

DAUPHINE.

She must consent, Sir Amorous, to reason.

LA FOOLE.

Why, she says they are no *decorum* among ladies.

OTTER.

But they are *decora*, and that's better, sir.

CLERIMONT.

Ay, she must hear argument. Did not Pasiphae, who was a   115
queen, love a bull? And was not Calisto, the mother of
Arcas, turn'd into a bear and made a star, Mistress Ursula,
i' the heavens?

OTTER.

Oh God, that I could ha' said as much! I will have these
stories painted i' the Bear Garden, *ex Ovidii Metamorphosi*.   120

DAUPHINE.

Where is your princess, Captain? Pray be our leader.

OTTER.

That I shall, sir.

CLERIMONT.

Make haste, good Sir Amorous.   [*Exeunt.*]

[III.iv]   [*Enter*] Morose, Epicoene, Parson, Cutbeard.

MOROSE.

Sir, there's an angel for yourself, and a brace of angels for
your cold. Muse not at this manage of my bounty. It is fit

---

114. *decora*] fine, graceful. Otter's pedantic joke, using the plural form.
116. *bull*] Jupiter in disguise.
117. *Ursula*] Jupiter's beloved, Calisto, was changed into the Great Bear
by Juno.
120. *ex Ovidii Metamorphosi*] out of Ovid's *Metamorphoses*.
[III.iv]
1. *angel*] a gold coin worth about ten shillings.

we should thank fortune, double to nature, for any benefit
she confers upon us; besides, it is your imperfection but my
solace.   5

PARSON.   *The* Parson *speaks as having a cold.*
I thank your worship, so is it mine now.

MOROSE.
What says he, Cutbeard?

CUTBEARD.
He says, *praesto*, sir, whensoever your worship needs him,
he can be ready with the like. He got this cold with sitting
up late and singing catches with cloth-workers.   10

MOROSE.
No more. I thank him.

PARSON.
God keep your worship and give you much joy with your
fair spouse. Umh, umh.   *He coughs.*

MOROSE.
Oh, oh, stay Cutbeard. Let him give me five shillings of my
money back. As it is bounty to reward benefits, so is it   15
equity to mulct injuries. I will have it. What says he?

CUTBEARD.
He cannot change it, sir.

MOROSE.
It must be chang'd.

CUTBEARD [*aside*].
Cough again.

MOROSE.
What says he?   20

CUTBEARD.
He will cough out the rest, sir.

PARSON.
Umh, umh, umh.   *Again.*

MOROSE.
Away, away with him, stop his mouth, away, I forgive it.—
                    [*Exit* Cutbeard *pushing the* Parson *before him.*]

---

3. *double to*] twice as much as we do to (Bald).
8. *praesto*] at your service.
  mulct] punish by imposing a fine.

EPICOENE.

> Fie, Master Morose, that you will use this violence to a man
> of the church. 25

MOROSE.

> How!

EPICOENE.

> It does not become your gravity or breeding (as you pretend
> in court) to have offered this outrage on a waterman or any
> more boist'rous creature, much less on a man of his civil
> coat. 30

MOROSE.

> You can speak then!

EPICOENE.

> Yes, sir.

MOROSE.

> Speak out I mean.

EPICOENE.

> Ay, sir. Why, did you think you had married a statue, or a
> motion only? One of the French puppets with the eyes 35
> turn'd with a wire? Or some innocent out of the hospital
> that would stand with her hands thus, and a plaise mouth,
> and look upon you.

MOROSE.

> Oh immodesty! A manifest woman! What, Cutbeard!

EPICOENE.

> Nay, never quarrel with Cutbeard, sir, it is too late now. I 40
> confess, it doth bate somewhat of the modesty I had when I
> writ simply maid; but I hope I shall make it a stock still
> competent to the estate and dignity of your wife.

MOROSE.

> She can talk!

---

28. *waterman*] a Thames boatman.

35. *motion*] puppet.

36. *innocent*] half-wit.

37. *hands thus*] possibly crossed hands, limply below the waist (see Edwin
Panofsky, *Life and Art of Dürer*, 4th ed., 1955, plates 43 and 256).

37. *plaise mouth*] turned down at the corners like a fish's mouth. *OED*
says "puckered mouth."

41. *bate*] abate, reduce.

43. *competent to*] a supply always sufficient to.

EPICOENE.

    Yes indeed, sir.   45

MOROSE.

    What, sirrah! None of my knaves there?

                    [*Enter* Mute.]

    Where is this impostor, Cutbeard?   [Mute *makes signs.*]

EPICOENE.

    Speak to him, fellow, speak to him. I'll have none of this
    coacted, unnatural dumbness in my house, in a family where
    I govern.   50

MOROSE.

    She is my regent already! I have married a Penthesilea, a
    Semiramis, sold my liberty to a distaffe!

[III.v]   [*Enter*] Truewit.

TRUEWIT.

    Where's Master Morose?

MOROSE.

    Is he come again! Lord have mercy upon me.

TRUEWIT.

    I wish you all joy, Mistress Epicoene, with your grave and
    honorable match.

EPICOENE.

    I return you the thanks, Master Truewit, so friendly a wish   5
    deserves.

MOROSE.

    She has acquaintance too!

TRUEWIT.

    God save you sir, and give you all contentment in your fair

0.1.] Truewit, Morose, Epicoene.
F1.

---

    49. *coacted*] compulsory.
    51. *Penthesilea*] queen of the Amazons.
    52. *Semiramis*] "A famous queen of Assyria . . . who, after the death
of her husband . . . fearing that the fierce people would be loth to be
governed by a woman, altered her apparel somewhat to the fashion of men
and took on the person of her son. [Later she] disclosed what she was, and
. . . at the last falling from nobleness to sensual lust, she desired the company of her son" (Cooper).

choice here. Before I was the bird of night to you, the owl,
but now I am the messenger of peace, a dove, and bring you   10
the glad wishes of many friends, to the celebration of this
good hour.

MOROSE.

What hour, sir?

TRUEWIT.

Your marriage hour, sir. I commend your resolution, that
(notwithstanding all the dangers I laid afore you in the   15
voice of a night-crow) would yet go on and be yourself.
It shews you are a man constant to your own ends, and
upright to your purposes, that would not be put off with left-
handed cries.

MOROSE.

How should you arrive at the knowledge of so much?   20

TRUEWIT.

Why, did you ever hope, sir, committing the secrecy of it
to a barber, that less than the whole town should know it?
You might as well ha' told it the conduit or the bakehouse
or the infantry that follow the court, and with more
security. Could your gravity forget so old and noted a rem-   25
nant as *lippis et tonsoribus notum*? Well, sir, forgive it yourself
now, the fault, and be communicable with your friends.
Here will be three or four fashionable ladies from the college
to visit you presently, and their train of minions and
followers.   30

MOROSE.

Bar my doors! Bar my doors! Where are all my eaters, my
mouths now?

[Enter Servants.]

Bar up my doors, you varlets.

EPICOENE.

He is a varlet that stirs to such an office. Let 'em stand

18–19. *left-handed*] sinister, ill-omened.

23. *conduit*] the fountain where water carriers and gossips assembled.

24. *infantry*] servants, who rode with the furniture and kitchen utensils
on royal progresses (H.S.).

25–26. *remnant*] quotation.

26. *lippis . . . notum*] "It is known to all, the bleary-eyed, and the barbers"
—i.e., purveyors of gossip (Horace *Satires* I.vii.3).

open. I would see him that dares move his eyes toward it. 35
Shall I have a barricado made against my friends, to be
barr'd of any pleasure they can bring in to me with honorable visitation?

MOROSE.

Oh Amazonian impudence!

TRUEWIT.

Nay, faith, in this, sir, she speaks but reason, and methinks 40
is more continent than you. Would you go to bed so
presently, sir, afore noon? A man of your head and hair
should owe more to that reverend ceremony, and not mount
the marriage-bed like a town bull or a mountain goat, but
stay the due season and ascend it then with religion and fear. 45
Those delights are to be steep'd in the humor and silence of
the night; and give the day to other open pleasures and
jollities of feast, of music, of revels, of discourse: we'll have
all, sir, that may make your Hymen high and happy.

MOROSE.

Oh, my torment, my torment! 50

TRUEWIT.

Nay, if you endure the first half hour, sir, so tediously,
and with this irksomeness, what comfort or hope can this
fair gentlewoman make to herself hereafter, in the con-
sideration of so many years as are to come—

MOROSE.

Of my affliction. Good sir, depart and let her do it alone. 55

TRUEWIT.

I have done, sir.

MOROSE.

That cursed barber!

TRUEWIT.

(Yes faith, a cursed wretch indeed, sir.)

38. visitation?] *followed by* "*Exeunt*   43. reverend] *MS correc. F1 (DFo6)*;
Ser." *Gifford.*   reveverend *F1.*

---

42. *head and hair*] intellect and character (*OED*).
49. *Hymen*] wedding.
58. (*Yes ... sir.*)] Jonson's parentheses here and in subsequent scenes
mark speeches in *sotto voce.*

MOROSE.

    I have married his cittern, that's common to all men.
Some plague, above the plague—   60

TRUEWIT.

    (All Egypt's ten plagues.)

MOROSE.

    Revenge me on him.

TRUEWIT.

    'Tis very well, sir. If you laid on a curse or two more,
I'll assure you he'll bear 'em. As, that he may get the
pox with seeking to cure it, sir? Or, that while he is   65
curling another man's hair, his own may drop off? Or, for
burning some male bawd's lock, he may have his brain
beat out with the curling iron?

MOROSE.

    No, let the wretch live wretched. May he get the itch and
his shop so lousy as no man dare come at him, nor he   70
come at no man.

TRUEWIT.

    (Ay, and if he would swallow all his balls for pills, let not
them purge him.)

MOROSE.

    Let his warming pan be ever cold.

TRUEWIT.

    (A perpetual frost underneath it, sir.)   75

MOROSE.

    Let him never hope to see fire again.

TRUEWIT.

    (But in hell, sir.)

MOROSE.

    His chairs be always empty, his scissors rust, and his
combs mould in their cases.

---

59. *cittern*] a lute-like instrument, often with the head of a woman
mounted on the peg box. They were available in barber shops, along with
virginals and lutes, for the customers to amuse themselves with (Kathleen
Schlesinger, *s.v.* Cittern, *Encyclopaedia Britannica*, 11th ed.).
    72. *balls*] of soap.

TRUEWIT.

Very dreadful that! (And may he lose the invention, sir, of   80
carving lanterns in paper.)

MOROSE.

Let there be no bawd carted that year to employ a basin of
his, but let him be glad to eat his sponge for bread.

TRUEWIT.

And drink lotium to it, and much good do him.

MOROSE.

Or, for want of bread—   85

TRUEWIT.

Eat earwax, sir. I'll help you. Or, draw his own teeth and
add them to the lute string.

MOROSE.

No, beat the old ones to powder and make bread of them.

TRUEWIT.

(Yes, make meal o' the millstones.)

MOROSE.

May all the botches and burns that he has cur'd on others   90
break out upon him.

TRUEWIT.

And he now forget the cure of 'em in himself, sir; or, if he do
remember it, let him ha' scrap'd all his linen into lint for't,
and have not a rag left him to set up with.

MOROSE.

Let him never set up again, but have the gout in his hands   95
forever. Now, no more, sir.

TRUEWIT.

Oh, that last was too high set! You might go less with
him i' faith, and be reveng'd enough; as, that he be never
able to new-paint his pole—

MOROSE.

Good sir, no more. I forgot myself.   100

---

81. *lanterns in paper*] sold at barber shops (cf. Jonson's *Tale of a Tub*,
V.vii.31–32).

82. *basin*] the crowd, watching a brothel keeper being carted through
the streets, beat on basins which barbers rented out (H.S.).

84. *lotium*] stale urine used by barbers to keep hair in place (*OED*).

86. *earwax . . . teeth*] barbers cleaned ears and pulled teeth, which they
hung on strings (H.S.).

TRUEWIT.

Or, want credit to take up with a combmaker—

MOROSE.

No more, sir.

TRUEWIT.

Or, having broken his glass in a former despair, fall now
into a much greater, of ever getting another—

MOROSE.

I beseech you, no more.   105

TRUEWIT.

Or, that he never be trusted with trimming of any but
chimney-sweepers—

MOROSE.

Sir—

TRUEWIT.

Or, may he cut a collier's throat with his razor by chance-
medley, and yet hang for't.   110

MOROSE.

I will forgive him, rather than hear any more. I beseech
you, sir.

[III.vi]

[*Enter*] Daw [*conducting*] Haughty, Centaur, Mavis, Trusty.

DAW.

This way, madam.

MOROSE.

Oh, the sea breaks in upon me! Another flood! An inun-
dation! I shall be o'erwhelm'd with noise. It beats already
at my shores. I feel an earthquake in myself for't.

DAW.

Give you joy, mistress.   5

MOROSE.

Has she servants too!

DAW.

I have brought some ladies here to see and know you.

0.1.] Daw,   Morose,   Truewit,
Haughty, Centaur, Mavis, Trusty.
F1.

109–110. *chance-medley*] manslaughter, "murder unaware" (*OED*).

She kisses them severally as he presents them.

My Lady Haughty, this my Lady Centaur, Mistress Dol
Mavis, Mistress Trusty my Lady Haughty's woman. Where's
your husband? Let's see him: can he endure no noise? Let   10
me come to him.

MOROSE.

What *nomenclator* is this!

TRUEWIT.

Sir John Daw, sir, your wife's servant, this.

MOROSE.

A Daw and her servant! Oh, 'tis decreed, 'tis decreed of me,
and she have such servants.   15

TRUEWIT.

Nay, sir, you must kiss the ladies, you must not go away
now; they come toward you to seek you out.

HAUGHTY.

I' faith, Master Morose, would you steal a marriage thus,
in the midst of so many friends and not acquaint us? Well,
I'll kiss you, notwithstanding the justice of my quarrel;   20
you shall give me leave, mistress, to use a becoming famili-
arity with your husband.

EPICOENE.

Your ladyship does me an honor in it, to let me know he is
so worthy your favor; as you have done both him and me
grace to visit so unprepar'd a pair to entertain you.   25

MOROSE.

Compliment! Compliment!

EPICOENE.

But I must lay the burden of that upon my servant here.

HAUGHTY.

It shall not need, Mistress Morose, we will all bear rather
than one shall be oppress'd.

MOROSE.

I know it, and you will teach her the faculty if she be to   30
learn it.

HAUGHTY [*whispering apart to the ladies and* Truewit].

Is this the silent woman?

---

12. *nomenclator*] announcer of guests' names; a pun on clatter.

CENTAUR.

> Nay, she has found her tongue since she was married, Master
> Truewit says.

HAUGHTY.

> Oh, Master Truewit! Save you. What kind of creature is   35
> your bride here? She speaks, methinks.

TRUEWIT.

> Yes, madam, believe it, she is a gentlewoman of very
> absolute behavior and of a good race.

HAUGHTY.

> And Jack Daw told us she could not speak.

TRUEWIT.

> So it was carried in plot, madam, to put her upon this   40
> old fellow, by Sir Dauphine, his nephew, and one or two
> more of us; but she is a woman of an excellent assurance,
> and an extraordinary happy wit and tongue. You shall see
> her make rare sport with Daw ere night.

HAUGHTY.

> And he brought us to laugh at her!   45

TRUEWIT.

> That falls out often, madam, that he that thinks himself
> the master-wit is the master-fool. I assure your ladyship, ye
> cannot laugh at her.

HAUGHTY.

> No, we'll have her to the college. And she have wit, she shall
> be one of us! Shall she not, Centaur? We'll make her a   50
> collegiate.

CENTAUR.

> Yes, faith, madam, and Mavis and she will set up a side.

TRUEWIT.

> Believe it, madam, and Mistress Mavis, she will sustain her
> part.

MAVIS.

> I'll tell you that when I have talk'd with her and tried her.   55

HAUGHTY.

> Use her very civilly, Mavis.

MAVIS.

> So I will, madam.

---

52. *set up a side*] act as partners in a game.

MOROSE.
Blessed minute, that they would whisper thus ever.

TRUEWIT.
In the meantime, madam, would but your ladyship help to
vex him a little: you know his disease, talk to him about   60
the wedding ceremonies or call for your gloves or—

HAUGHTY.
Let me alone. Centaur, help me. —Master bridegroom,
where are you?

MOROSE.
Oh, it was too miraculously good to last!

HAUGHTY.
We see no ensigns of a wedding here, no character of a   65
bride-ale: where be our scarves and our gloves? I pray
you, give 'em us. Let's know your bride's colors and yours
at least.

CENTAUR.
Alas, madam, he has provided none.

MOROSE.
Had I known your ladyship's painter, I would.   70

HAUGHTY.
He has given it you, Centaur, i' faith. But do you hear,
Master Morose, a jest will not absolve you in this manner.
You that have suck'd the milk of the court and from thence
have been brought up to the very strong meats and wine of
it, been a courtier from the biggen to the nightcap (as we   75
may say), and you to offend in such a high point of ceremony as this, and let your nuptials want all marks of
solemnity! How much plate have you lost today (if you
had but regarded your profit), what gifts, what friends,
through your mere rusticity?   80

MOROSE.
Madam—

---

61. *gloves*] presented to ladies at weddings.
65. *ensigns*] signs.
67. *colors*] colors of coats of arms displayed at fancy weddings by tilters
(H.S.).
70. *painter*] i.e., her cosmetician.
75. *biggen*] baby's bonnet.

4   –73–

HAUGHTY.

> Pardon me, sir, I must insinuate your errors to you. No
> gloves? no garters? no scarves? no epithalamium? no
> mask?

DAW.

> Yes, madam, I'll make an epithalamium, I promis'd my   85
> mistress, I have begun it already: will your ladyship hear it?

HAUGHTY.

> Ay, good Jack Daw.

MOROSE [*to* Lady Haughty].

> Will it please your ladyship command a chamber and be
> private with your friend? You shall have your choice of
> rooms to retire to after; my whole house is yours. I know   90
> it hath been your ladyship's errand into the city at other
> times, however now you have been unhappily diverted upon
> me; but I shall be loath to break any honorable custom of
> your ladyship's. And therefore, good madam—

EPICOENE.

> Come, you are a rude bridegroom to entertain ladies of   95
> honor in this fashion.

CENTAUR.

> He is a rude groom, indeed.

TRUEWIT.

> By that light, you deserve to be grafted and have your
> horns reach from one side of the island to the other. —Do
> not mistake me, sir. I but speak this to give the ladies some 100
> heart again, not for any malice to you.

MOROSE.

> Is this your bravo, ladies?

TRUEWIT.

> As God help me, if you utter such another word, I'll take
> mistress bride in and begin to you in a very sad cup, do
> you see? Go to, know your friends and such as love you.   105

104. to] *Gifford;* too *F1.*

---

91. *errand*] purpose to go.
98. *grafted*] cuckolded.
102. *bravo*] bully, hired assassin.
104. *sad cup*] in a seriously painful way.

[III.vii]   [*Enter*] Clerimont [*leading a number of musicians*].

CLERIMONT.

    By your leave, ladies. Do you want any music? I have
brought you variety of noises. Play, sirs, all of you.

MOROSE.   *Music of all sorts.*

    Oh, a plot, a plot, a plot, a plot upon me! This day I shall
be their anvil to work on, they will grate me asunder.
'Tis worse than the noise of a saw.   5

CLERIMONT.

    No, they are hair, rosin, and guts. I can give you the
receipt.

TRUEWIT.

    Peace, boys.

CLERIMONT.

    Play, I say.

TRUEWIT.

    Peace rascals. [*To* Morose.] You see who's your   10
friend now, sir? Take courage, put on a martyr's resolution. Mock down all their attemptings with patience.
'Tis but a day, and I would suffer heroically. Should an ass
exceed me in fortitude? No. You betray your infirmity with
your hanging dull ears, and make them insult: bear up   15
bravely and constantly.

La Foole *passes over sewing the meat* [*with servants, followed by* Mrs. Otter].

    Look you here, sir, what honor is done you unexpected by
your nephew; a wedding dinner come and a Knight-sewer
before it, for the more reputation, and fine Mistress Otter,
your neighbor, in the rump or tail of it.   20

MOROSE.

    Is that Gorgon, that Medusa come? Hide me, hide me.

TRUEWIT.

    I warrant you, sir, she will not transform you. Look upon
her with a good courage. Pray you entertain her and conduct

0.1.] Clerimont, Morose, Truewit,
Dauphine, La Foole, Otter, Mrs.
Otter. &c. *F1.*

16.1. *sewing*] carrying.
22. *transform*] into stone, as the head of Medusa did.

your guests in. No? —Mistress bride, will you entreat in
the ladies? Your bridegroom is so shamefac'd, here—   25

EPICOENE.

Will it please your ladyship, madam?

HAUGHTY.

With the benefit of your company, mistress.

EPICOENE.

Servant, pray you perform your duties.

DAW.

And glad to be commanded, mistress.

CENTAUR.

How like you her wit, Mavis?   30

MAVIS.

Very prettily, absolutely well.

MRS. OTTER.

'Tis my place.   [*Trying to take precedence.*]

MAVIS.

You shall pardon me, Mistress Otter.

MRS. OTTER.

Why, I am a collegiate.

MAVIS.

But not in ordinary.   35

MRS. OTTER.

But I am.

MAVIS.

We'll dispute that within.   [*Exeunt ladies.*]

CLERIMONT.

Would this had lasted a little longer.

TRUEWIT.

And that they had sent for the heralds.

[*Enter* Captain Otter.]

Captain Otter, what news?   40

OTTER.

I have brought my bull, bear, and horse in private, and
yonder are the trumpeters without, and the drum, gentlemen.

MOROSE.

Oh, oh, oh.   *The drum and trumpets sound.*

---

39. *heralds*] who determined questions of precedence.

In ordinary: regular member of staff or class.

OTTER.

And we will have a rouse in each of 'em anon, for bold 45
Britons, i' faith.   [*They sound again.*]

MOROSE.

Oh, oh, oh.   [*Exit* Morose.]

ALL.

Follow, follow, follow.   [*Exeunt.*]

[IV.i]   [*Enter*] Truewit, Clerimont.

TRUEWIT.

Was there ever poor bridegroom so tormented? or man
indeed?

CLERIMONT.

I have not read of the like in the chronicles of the land.

TRUEWIT.

Sure, he cannot but go to a place of rest after all this
purgatory.   5

CLERIMONT.

He may presume it, I think.

TRUEWIT.

The spitting, the coughing, the laughter, the neezing, the
farting, dancing, noise of the music, and her masculine
and loud commanding, and urging the whole family,
makes him think he has married a fury.   10

CLERIMONT.

And she carries it up bravely.

TRUEWIT.

Ay, she takes any occasion to speak: that's the height on't.

CLERIMONT.

And how soberly Dauphine labors to satisfy him that it was
none of his plot!

TRUEWIT.

And has almost brought him to the faith i' the article.   15

0.1.] Truewit, Clerimont, Dauphine. *F1.*

---

45. *rouse*] deep drink.
[IV.i]
7. *neezing*] sneezing.
9. *family*] household (Bald).

[*Enter* Dauphine.]

Here he comes. —Where is he now? What's become of
him, Dauphine?

DAUPHINE.

Oh, hold me up a little, I shall go away i' the jest else.
He has got on his whole nest of nightcaps, and lock'd himself up i' the top o' the house, as high as ever he can climb   20
from the noise. I peep'd in at a cranny and saw him sitting
over a crossbeam o' the roof, like him o' the saddler's horse
in Fleet Street, upright; and he will sleep there.

CLERIMONT.

But where are your collegiates?

DAUPHINE.

Withdrawn with the bride in private.   25

TRUEWIT.

Oh, they are instructing her i' the college-grammar. If she
have grace with them, she knows all their secrets instantly.

CLERIMONT.

Methinks the Lady Haughty looks well today, for all my
dispraise of her i' the morning. I think I shall come about
to thee again, Truewit.   30

TRUEWIT.

Believe it, I told you right. Women ought to repair the
losses time and years have made i' their features, with
dressings. And an intelligent woman, if she know by herself the least defect, will be most curious to hide it, and it
becomes her. If she be short, let her sit much, lest when she   35
stands she be thought to sit. If she have an ill foot, let her
wear her gown the longer and her shoe the thinner. If a
fat hand and scal'd nails, let her carve the less, and act in
gloves. If a sour breath, let her never discourse fasting, and
always talk at her distance. If she have black and rugged   40

---

22. *saddler's horse*] a dummy in front of a shop.
33. *by*] concerning.
34. *curious*] careful.
38. *scal'd*] scabbed, hence scurvy or mean.
38. *carve*] make affected or "apish motions with the hands," according
to Littleton's *Latin English lexicon,* 1675 (H.S.).
38. *act*] gesture.

teeth, let her offer the less at laughter, especially if she
laugh wide and open.

CLERIMONT.

Oh, you shall have some women, when they laugh, you
would think they bray'd, it is so rude, and—

TRUEWIT.

Ay, and others that will stalk i' their gait like an estrich,   45
and take huge strides. I cannot endure such a sight. I love
measure i' the feet and number i' the voice: they are
gentlenesses that ofttimes draw no less than the face.

DAUPHINE.

How cam'st thou to study these creatures so exactly? I would
thou would'st make me a proficient.   50

TRUEWIT.

Yes, but you must leave to live i' your chamber then a
month together upon *Amadis de Gaul* or *Don Quixote*, as you
are wont, and come abroad where the matter is frequent, to
court, to tiltings, public shows and feasts, to plays and
church sometimes: thither they come to show their new   55
tires too, to see and to be seen. In these places a man shall
find whom to love, whom to play with, whom to touch once,
whom to hold ever. The variety arrests his judgment. A
wench to please a man comes not down dropping from the
ceiling, as he lies on his back droning a tobacco pipe. He   60
must go where she is.

DAUPHINE.

Yes, and be never the near.

TRUEWIT.

Out, heretic. That diffidence makes thee worthy it should
be so.

---

45. *estrich*] ostrich.   47. *measure*] grace.
47. *number*] rhythm.   51. *leave*] cease.
52. *Amadis de Gaul*] the most popular of chivalric romances; first published 1508, the English translation *c.* 1590.
52. *Don Quixote*] one of the earliest allusions in English to Cervantes'
masterpiece. If the allusion was in the script of 1609, the book was popular
before its English translation, 1612 (James Fitzmaurice-Kelly, "Cervantes
in England," *British Academy, Proceedings*, II, 18).
60. *droning*] sucking at, as if playing a bagpipe.
62. *near*] nearer.

CLERIMONT.

He says true to you, Dauphine.   65

DAUPHINE.

Why?

TRUEWIT.

A man should not doubt to overcome any woman. Think
he can vanquish 'em and he shall; for though they deny,
their desire is to be tempted. Penelope herself cannot hold
out long. Ostend, you saw, was taken at last. You must   70
persevere and hold to your purpose. They would solicit us,
but that they are afraid. Howsoever, they wish in their hearts
we should solicit them. Praise 'em, flatter 'em, you shall
never want eloquence or trust; even the chastest delight to
feel themselves that way rubb'd. With praises you must mix   75
kisses too. If they take them, they'll take more. Though
they strive, they would be overcome.

CLERIMONT.

Oh, but a man must beware of force.

TRUEWIT.

It is to them an acceptable violence, and has ofttimes the
place of the greatest courtesy. She that might have been   80
forc'd, and you let her go free without touching, though
she then seem to thank you, will ever hate you after; and
glad i' the face, is assuredly sad at the heart.

CLERIMONT.

But all women are not to be taken all ways.

TRUEWIT.

'Tis true. No more than all birds or all fishes. If you appear   85
learned to an ignorant wench, or jocund to a sad, or witty
to a foolish, why she presently begins to mistrust herself.
You must approach them i' their own height, their own line;
for the contrary makes many that fear to commit themselves to noble and worthy fellows, run into the embraces   90
of a rascal. If she love wit, give verses, though you borrow
'em of a friend or buy 'em to have good. If valor, talk of

84. all ways] *Whalley;* alwaies *F1.*

---

70. *Ostend*] Belgian port besieged by the Spanish from July, 1601, to
September, 1604.
83. *glad . . . heart*] a proverb (Tilley, F 3).

your sword and be frequent in the mention of quarrels,
though you be staunch in fighting. If activity, be seen o'
your barbary often, or leaping over stools for the credit of   95
your back. If she love good clothes or dressing, have your
learned council about you every morning, your French
tailor, barber, linener, *et cetera*. Let your powder, your
glass, and your comb be your dearest acquaintance. Take
more care for the ornament of your head than the safety,   100
and wish the commonwealth rather troubled than a hair
about you. That will take her. Then if she be covetous and
craving, do you promise anything and perform sparingly;
so shall you keep her in appetite still. Seem as you would
give but be like a barren field that yields little, or unlucky 105
dice to foolish and hoping gamesters. Let your gifts be slight
and dainty rather than precious. Let cunning be above cost.
Give cherries at time of year, or apricots; and say they were
sent you out o' the country, though you bought 'em in Cheapside. Admire her tires, like her in all fashions, compare her in 110
every habit to some deity, invent excellent dreams to flatter
her, and riddles; or, if she be a great one, perform always
the second parts to her: like what she likes, praise whom she
praises, and fail not to make the household and servants
yours, yea the whole family, and salute 'em by their names 115
('tis but light cost if you can purchase 'em so), and make
her physician your pensioner, and her chief woman. Nor
will it be out of your gain to make love to her too, so she
follow, not usher, her lady's pleasure. All blabbing is taken
away when she comes to be a part of the crime.   120

DAUPHINE.

On what courtly lap hast thou late slept, to come forth so
sudden and absolute a courtling?

TRUEWIT.

Good faith, I should rather question you that are so hark'n-
ing after these mysteries. I begin to suspect your diligence,
Dauphine. Speak, art thou in love in earnest?   125

98. *et cetera*] &c. *Fl.*

---

98. *staunch*] restrained.   95. *barbary*] horse.
95. *leaping*] cf. V.i.39.   107. *cunning*] dexterity, ingenuity.
122. *courtling*] courtier.

DAUPHINE.

Yes, by my troth am I; 'twere ill dissembling before thee.

TRUEWIT.

With which of 'em, I pray thee?

DAUPHINE.

With all the collegiates.

CLERIMONT.

Out on thee. We'll keep you at home, believe it, i' the
stable, and you be such a stallion.   130

TRUEWIT.

No. I like him well. Men should love wisely, and all women:
some one for the face, and let her please the eye; another for
the skin, and let her please the touch; a third for the voice,
and let her please the ear; and where the objects mix, let
the senses so too. Thou wouldst think it strange if I should 135
make 'em all in love with thee afore night!

DAUPHINE.

I would say thou hadst the best philter i' the world, and
couldst do more than Madam Medea or Doctor Foreman.

TRUEWIT.

If I do not, let me play the mountebank for my meat while I
live, and the bawd for my drink.   140

DAUPHINE.

So be it, I say.

[IV.ii]   [*Enter*] Otter, Daw, La Foole.

OTTER.

Oh lord, gentlemen, how my knights and I have miss'd you
here!

CLERIMONT.

Why, captain, what service? what service?

0.1.] Otter, Clerimont, Daw, Dauphine, Morose, Truewit, La Foole,
Mrs. Otter. *F1.*

---

138. *Medea*] "by her sorcery restored to young years again [Jason's]
old father Aeson" (Cooper).

138. *Doctor Foreman*] astrologer and quack who was thought to have
supplied love-philters to women.

OTTER.

To see me bring up my bull, bear, and horse to fight.

DAW.

Yes, faith, the captain says we shall be his dogs to bait 'em.   5

DAUPHINE.

A good employment.

TRUEWIT.

Come on, let's see a course then.

LA FOOLE.

I am afraid my cousin will be offended if she come.

OTTER.

Be afraid of nothing. —Gentlemen, I have plac'd the drum
and the trumpets and one to give 'em the sign when you   10
are ready. [*Brings out his cups.*] Here's my bull for myself,
and my bear for Sir John Daw, and my horse for Sir
Amorous. Now set your foot to mine and yours to his, and—

LA FOOLE.

Pray God my cousin come not.

OTTER.

Saint George and Saint Andrew, fear no cousins. Come,   15
sound, sound. *Et rauco strepuerunt cornua cantu.*

[*Drum and trumpets sound. They drink.*]

TRUEWIT.

Well said, captain, i' faith: well fought at the bull.

CLERIMONT.

Well held at the bear.

TRUEWIT.

Low, low, captain.

DAUPHINE.

Oh, the horse has kick'd off his dog already.   20

LA FOOLE.

I cannot drink it, as I am a knight.

TRUEWIT.

Gods so, off with his spurs, somebody.

LA FOOLE.

It goes again my conscience. My cousin will be angry with it.

---

7. *course*] a round, a series.
16. *Et . . . cantu*] "And the horns blared out with a hoarse sound"
(Virgil *Aeneid* viii.2).

15! as in 'no colours'   –83–

DAW.

> I ha' done mine.

TRUEWIT.

> You fought high and fair, Sir John.   25

CLERIMONT.

> At the head.

DAUPHINE.

> Like an excellent bear-dog.

CLERIMONT [*apart to* Daw].

> You take no notice of the business, I hope.

DAW.

> Not a word, sir, you see we are jovial.

OTTER.

> Sir Amorous, you must not equivocate. It must be pull'd   30
> down, for all my cousin.

CLERIMONT [*apart to* La Foole].

> 'Sfoot, if you take not your drink, they'll think you are
> discontented with something: you'll betray all if you take the
> least notice.

LA FOOLE.

> Not I, I'll both drink and talk then.   35

OTTER.

> You must pull the horse on his knees, Sir Amorous: fear
> no cousins. *Jacta est alea.*

TRUEWIT.

> Oh, now he's in his vein, and bold. The least hint given him
> of his wife now will make him rail desperately.

CLERIMONT.

> Speak to him of her.   40

TRUEWIT.

> Do you, and I'll fetch her to the hearing of it.   [*Exit.*]

DAUPHINE.

> Captain he-Otter, your she-Otter is coming, your wife.

OTTER.

> Wife! Buz. *Titivilitium.* There's no such thing in nature. I
> confess, gentlemen, I have a cook, a laundress, a house-
> drudge, that serves my necessary turns and goes under that   45

---

37. *Jacta est alea*] The die is cast: Caesar's remark as he crossed the
Rubicon.
43. *Titivilitium*] "A vile thing of no value. Another thread" (Cooper).

title; but he's an ass that will be so uxorious to tie his
affections to one circle. Come, the name dulls appetite. Here,
replenish again: another bout. Wives are nasty sluttish
animals—   [*Fills the cups again.*]

DAUPHINE.

Oh, captain.   50

OTTER.

As ever the earth bare, *tribus verbis*. Where's Master Truewit?

DAW.

He's slipp'd aside, sir.

CLERIMONT.

But you must drink and be jovial.

DAW.

Yes, give it me.

LA FOOLE.

And me, too.   55

DAW.

Let's be jovial.

LA FOOLE.

As jovial as you will.

OTTER.

Agreed. Now you shall ha' the bear, cousin, and Sir John
Daw the horse, and I'll ha' the bull still. Sound Tritons o'
the Thames. *Nunc est bibendum, nunc pede libero*—   60

MOROSE (*speaks from above* [*within*]: *the trumpets sounding*).

Villains, murderers, sons of the earth, and traitors, what
do you there?

CLERIMONT.

Oh, now the trumpets have wak'd him we shall have his
company.

OTTER.

A wife is a scurvy *clogdogdo*, an unlucky thing, a very fore-   65
said bear whelp, without any good fashion or breeding:
mala bestia.

---

51. *tribus verbis*] "briefly, in three words" (Cooper).

60. *Nunc . . . libero*] "Now it is time to drink, now with free foot" (Horace
Odes I.xxxvii.1).

65. *clogdogdo*] meaning uncertain; possibly Bear Garden slang for a
"clog proper only for a dog" (Upton, *Remarks on Three Plays of Ben Jonson*,
1749, pp. 59–94).

65–66. *very foresaid*] truly predictable, certain to be bad.

67. *mala bestia*] evil beast.

His wife is brought out [by Truewit] *to hear him [unobserved].*

DAUPHINE.

Why did you marry one then, captain?

OTTER.

A pox—I married with six thousand pound, ay. I was in
love with that. I ha' not kiss'd my fury these forty   70
weeks.

CLERIMONT.

The more to blame you, captain.

TRUEWIT.

Nay, Mistress Otter, hear him a little first.

OTTER.

She has a breath worse than my grandmother's, *profecto.*

MRS. OTTER.

Oh treacherous liar. Kiss me, sweet Master Truewit, and   75
prove him a slandering knave.

TRUEWIT.

I'll rather believe you, lady.

OTTER.

And she has a peruke that's like a pound of hemp made up
in shoe-threads.

MRS. OTTER.

Oh viper, mandrake!   80

OTTER.

A most vile face! And yet she spends me forty pound a year
in mercury and hogs-bones. All her teeth were made i' the
Blackfriars, both her eyebrows i' the Strand, and her hair
in Silver Street. Every part o' the town owns a piece
of her.   85

MRS. OTTER.

I cannot hold.

OTTER.

She takes herself asunder still when she goes to bed, into
some twenty boxes, and about next day noon is put together
again, like a great German clock; and so comes forth and
rings a tedious larum to the whole house, and then is quiet 90

---

74. *profecto*] truly.
82. *mercury and hogs-bones*] ingredients of cosmetics.
90. *larum*] uproar.

again for an hour, but for her quarters. —Ha' you done me
right gentlemen?

MRS. OTTER.

(*She falls upon him and beats him.*) No, sir, I'll do you right
with my quarters, with my quarters.

OTTER.

Oh, hold, good princess.   95

TRUEWIT.

Sound, sound.   [*Drum and trumpets sound.*]

CLERIMONT.

A battle, a battle.

MRS. OTTER.

You notorious stinkardly bearward, does my breath smell?

OTTER.

Under correction, dear princess: look to my bear and my
horse, gentlemen.   100

MRS. OTTER.

Do I want teeth and eyebrows, thou bulldog?

TRUEWIT.

Sound, sound still.   [*They sound again.*]

OTTER.

No, I protest, under correction—

MRS. OTTER.

Ay, now you are under correction, you protest; but you did
not protest before correction, sir. Thou Judas, to offer to 105
betray thy princess! I'll make thee an example—

Morose *descends with a long sword.*

MOROSE.

I will have no such examples in my house, Lady Otter.

MRS. OTTER.

Ah—

MOROSE.

Mistress Mary Ambree, your examples are dangerous.—
                    [Mrs. Otter, Daw, La Foole *run off.*]
Rogues, hellhounds, Stentors, out of my doors, you sons of 110

---

109. *Mary Ambree*] according to a ballad, she disguised herself as a
soldier at the siege of Ghent in 1584.

noise and tumult, begot on an ill May-day, or when the
galley-foist is afloat to Westminster! [*Drives out the musicians.*]
A trumpeter could not be conceiv'd but then.

DAUPHINE.

What ails you, sir?

MOROSE.

They have rent my roof, walls, and all my windores asunder,   115
with their brazen throats.   [*Exit.*]

TRUEWIT.

Best follow him, Dauphine.

DAUPHINE.

So I will.   [*Exit.*]

CLERIMONT.

Where's Daw and La Foole?

OTTER.

They are both run away, sir. Good gentlemen, help to pacify   120
my princess, and speak to the great ladies for me. Now must
I go lie with the bears this fortnight, and keep out o' the way
till my peace be made, for this scandal she has taken. Did
you not see my bullhead, gentlemen?

CLERIMONT.

Is't not on, captain?   125

TRUEWIT.

No, but he may make a new one, by that is on.

OTTER.

Oh, here 'tis. And you come over, gentlemen, and ask for
Tom Otter, we'll go down to Ratcliff and have a course i'
faith, for all these disasters. There's *bona spes* left.

TRUEWIT.

Away, captain, get off while you are well.   [*Exit* Otter.] 130

---

111. *ill May-day*] proverbial; day of the riot in London in 1517, against
foreigners.

112. *galley-foist*] state barge in which the Lord Mayor went to Westminster to be sworn in.

123. *scandal*] offence.

128. *Ratcliff*] a suburb of London, on the Thames, where rogues hid
out.

129. *bona spes*] "*Omnium rerum desperatione confligit bona spes*, Cicero [*Catiline*,
II.25]. Good hope striveth with despair of all things" (Cooper).

CLERIMONT.
I am glad we are rid of him.
TRUEWIT.
You had never been, unless we had put his wife upon him.
His humor is as tedious at last as it was ridiculous at first.

[IV.iii]
[*Enter*] Haughty, Mrs. Otter, Mavis, Daw, La Foole, Centaur,
Epicoene; Truewit [and] Clerimont [*observing*].

HAUGHTY.
We wonder'd why you shriek'd so, Mistress Otter.
MRS. OTTER.
Oh God, madam, he came down with a huge long naked
weapon in both his hands, and look'd so dreadfully! Sure,
he's beside himself.
MAVIS.
Why, what made you there, Mistress Otter?   5
MRS. OTTER.
Alas, Mistress Mavis, I was chastising my subject, and
thought nothing of him.
DAW.
Faith, mistress, you must do so too. Learn to chastise.
Mistress Otter corrects her husband so, he dares not speak
but under correction.   10
LA FOOLE.
And with his hat off to her: 'twould do you good to see.
HAUGHTY.
In sadness 'tis good and mature counsel: practice it, Morose.
I'll call you Morose still now, as I call Centaur and Mavis:
we four will be all one.
CENTAUR.
And you'll come to the college and live with us?   15

133. first.] *followed by* "*Exeunt.*"
Gifford.

12. *In sadness*] seriously.
13. *Morose*] i.e., use the masculine form of address. "The Countess of
Bedford, Jonson's patron, addressed Lady Cornwallis in fifteen extant
letters as 'Dear Cornwallis'" (H.S.).

ʜᴀᴜɢʜᴛʏ.

Make him give milk and honey.

ᴍᴀᴠɪꜱ.

Look how you manage him at first, you shall have him ever after.

ᴄᴇɴᴛᴀᴜʀ.

Let him allow you your coach and four horses, your woman, your chambermaid, your page, your gentleman-usher, your   20
French cook, and four grooms.

ʜᴀᴜɢʜᴛʏ.

And go with us to Bedlam, to the china-houses, and to the Exchange.

ᴄᴇɴᴛᴀᴜʀ.

It will open the gate to your fame.

ʜᴀᴜɢʜᴛʏ.

Here's Centaur has immortaliz'd herself with taming of her   25
wild male.

ᴍᴀᴠɪꜱ.

Ay, she has done the miracle of the kingdom.

ᴇᴘɪᴄᴏᴇɴᴇ.

But ladies, do you count it lawful to have such plurality of servants, and do 'em all graces?

ʜᴀᴜɢʜᴛʏ.

Why not? Why should women deny their favors to men?   30
Are they the poorer or the worse?

ᴅᴀᴡ.

Is the Thames the less for the dyers' water, mistress?

ʟᴀ ꜰᴏᴏʟᴇ.

Or a torch for lighting many torches?

ᴛʀᴜᴇᴡɪᴛ.

Well said, La Foole; what a new one he has got!

27.] *followed by S.D.: Enter* Clerimont *and* Truewit. *Gifford.*

---

22. *Bedlam*] Bethlehem Hospital for the insane. See Dekker's *Honest Whore*, Part I, V.ii, for a typical visit, when various types of madmen are exhibited for the company.

32. *dyers' water*] a variation on the proverb "To cast water into the Thames" (Tilley, W 106).

33. *torch . . . torches*] a proverb (Tilley, C 45).

CENTAUR.

They are empty losses women fear in this kind.   35

HAUGHTY.

Besides, ladies should be mindful of the approach of age,
and let no time want his due use. The best of our days pass
first.

MAVIS.

We are rivers that cannot be call'd back, madam: she that
now excludes her lovers may live to lie a forsaken beldame   40
in a frozen bed.

CENTAUR.

'Tis true, Mavis; and who will wait on us to coach then, or
write, or tell us the news then? Make anagrams of our names,
and invite us to the Cockpit and kiss our hands all the play-
time, and draw their weapons for our honors?   45

HAUGHTY.

Not one.

DAW.

Nay, my mistress is not altogether unintelligent of these
things; here be in presence have tasted of her favors.

CLERIMONT.

What a neighing hobbyhorse is this!

EPICOENE.

But not with intent to boast 'em again, servant. And have   50
you those excellent receipts, madam, to keep yourselves from
bearing of children?

HAUGHTY.

Oh yes, Morose. How should we maintain our youth and
beauty else? Many births of a woman make her old, as many
crops make the earth barren.   55

[IV.iv]   [*Enter*] Morose, Dauphine.

MOROSE.

Oh my cursed angel, that instructed me to this fate!

0.1.] Morose, Dauphine, Truewit,   Haughty, La Foole, Centaur, Mavis,
Epicoene, Clerimont, Daw,   Mrs. Otter, Trusty. *F1.*

37–38. *best . . . first*] a proverb (Tilley, B 318).
44. *the Cockpit*] a theater in Whitehall.

DAUPHINE.

Why, sir?

MOROSE.

That I should be seduc'd by so foolish a devil as a barber
will make!

DAUPHINE.

I would I had been worthy, sir, to have partaken your   5
counsel; you should never have trusted it to such a minister.

MOROSE.

Would I could redeem it with the loss of an eye, nephew,
a hand, or any other member.

DAUPHINE.

Marry, God forbid, sir, that you should geld yourself to
anger your wife.   10

MOROSE.

So it would rid me of her! And that I did supererogatory
penance in a belfry at Westminster Hall, i' the Cockpit, at
the fall of a stag, the Tower Wharf (what place is there
else?), London Bridge, Paris Garden, Billingsgate, when the
noises are at their height and loudest. Nay, I would sit out   15
a play that were nothing but fights at sea, drum, trumpet,
and target!

DAUPHINE.

I hope there shall be no such need, sir. Take patience, good
uncle. This is but a day, and 'tis well worn too now.

MOROSE.

Oh, 'twill be so forever, nephew, I foresee it, forever.   20
Strife and tumult are the dowry that comes with a wife.

TRUEWIT.

I told you so, sir, and you would not believe me.

MOROSE.

Alas, do not rub those wounds, Master Truewit, to blood

12. i' the Cockpit] *F1 (corr.)*; in a
Cock-pit *F1 (uncorr.)*.

---

12. *i' the Cockpit*] the press correction (see textual note) alters the passage
from a general reference to the particular arena where cock fights and plays
were performed.

13. *fall of a stag*] when horns of the huntsmen sounded the death of the
deer.

17. *target*] shield.

again; 'twas my negligence. Add not affliction to affliction.
I have perceiv'd the effect of it, too late, in Madam Otter.   25

EPICOENE.

How do you, sir?

MOROSE.

Did you ever hear a more unnecessary question? As if she
did not see! Why, I do as you see, empress, empress.

EPICOENE.

You are not well, sir! You look very ill! Something has
distempered you.   30

MOROSE.

Oh horrible, monstrous impertinencies! Would not one of
these have serv'd? Do you think, sir, would not one of these
have serv'd?

TRUEWIT.

Yes, sir, but these are but notes of female kindness, sir:
certain tokens that she has a voice, sir.   35

MOROSE.

Oh, is't so? Come, and't be no otherwise— What say you?

EPICOENE.

How do you feel yourself, sir?

MOROSE.

Again that!

TRUEWIT.

Nay, look you, sir: you would be friends with your wife
upon unconscionable terms, her silence—   40

EPICOENE.

They say you are run mad, sir.

MOROSE.

Not for love, I assure you, of you; do you see?

EPICOENE.

Oh lord, gentlemen! Lay hold on him for God's sake: what
shall I do? Who's his physician (can you tell) that knows
the state of his body best, that I might send for him? Good   45
sir, speak. I'll send for one of my doctors else.

MOROSE.

What, to poison me, that I might die intestate and leave
you possess'd of all?

EPICOENE.

Lord, how idly he talks, and how his eyes sparkle! He looks

green about the temples! Do you see what blue spots he has?   50

CLERIMONT.

Ay, it's melancholy.

EPICOENE.

Gentlemen, for heaven's sake counsel me. Ladies! Servant,
you have read Pliny and Paracelsus. Ne'er a word now to
comfort a poor gentlewoman? Ay me! What fortune had I to
marry a distracted man?   55

DAW.

I'll tell you, mistress—

TRUEWIT [aside].

How rarely she holds it up!

MOROSE.

What mean you, gentlemen?

EPICOENE.

What will you tell me, servant?

DAW.

The disease in Greek is called μανία, in Latin *insania, furor,*   60
vel ecstasis melancholica, that is, *egressio,* when a man *ex
melancholico evadit fanaticus.*

MOROSE.

Shall I have a lecture read upon me alive?

DAW.

But he may be but *phreneticus* yet, mistress, and *phrenetis* is
only *delirium* or so—   65

EPICOENE.

Ay, that is for the disease, servant; but what is this to the
cure? We are sure enough of the disease.

MOROSE.

Let me go.

---

51. *melancholy*] neurosis. Wits, poets, courtiers, and travelers back from
Italy became fashionably melancholic and were interested in books on
curing it.

53. *Pliny and Paracelsus*] who wrote on natural history and medicine,
respectively, an ancient and a modern.

60. *μανία*] mania.

60–62. *insania . . . fanaticus*] insanity, madness, or melancholic ecstasy,
that is, a losing of his wits, when a man from a melancholy state becomes
mad. Daw distinguishes it from melancholy.

TRUEWIT.

Why, we'll entreat her to hold her peace, sir.

MOROSE.

Oh no. Labor not to stop her. She is like a conduit-pipe   70
that will gush out with more force when she opens again.

HAUGHTY.

I'll tell you Morose, you must talk divinity to him altogether, or moral philosophy.

LA FOOLE.

Ay, and there's an excellent book of moral philosophy,
madam, of Reynard the Fox and all the beasts, call'd *Doni's*   75
Philosophy.

CENTAUR.

There is, indeed, Sir Amorous La Foole.

MOROSE.

Oh misery!

LA FOOLE.

I have read it, my Lady Centaur, all over to my cousin
here.   80

MRS. OTTER.

Ay, and 'tis a very good book as any is of the moderns.

DAW.

Tut, he must have Seneca read to him, and Plutarch and the
ancients; the moderns are not for this disease.

CLERIMONT.

Why, you discommended them too, today, Sir John.

DAW.

Ay, in some cases; but in these they are best, and Aristotle's   85
Ethics.

MAVIS.

Say you so, Sir John? I think you are deceiv'd: you took it
upon trust.

HAUGHTY.

Where's Trusty, my woman? I'll end this difference. I

75–76. *Doni's Philosophy*] an ancient collection of *Fables of Bidpai*, trans-
lated in Italian by Doni and into English by Thomas North (1570). Sir
Amorous has confused it with the medieval fable of *Reynard the Fox*.

83. *moderns . . . disease*] early interest in the controversy over the value of
ancient and modern writers, climaxed in Swift's *Battle of the Books* (1704).

prithee, Otter, call her. Her father and mother were both 90
mad when they put her to me. [*Exit* Mrs. Otter.]

MOROSE.

I think so. —Nay, gentlemen, I am tame. This is but an
exercise, I know, a marriage ceremony, which I must
endure.

HAUGHTY.

And one of 'em (I know not which) was cur'd with *The* 95
Sick Man's Salve, and the other with *Green's Groats-worth of*
Wit.

TRUEWIT.

A very cheap cure, madam.

HAUGHTY.

Ay, it's very feasible.

[*Enter* Mrs. Otter *with* Trusty.]

MRS. OTTER.

My lady call'd for you, Mistress Trusty: you must decide a 100
controversy.

HAUGHTY.

Oh, Trusty, which was it you said, your father or your
mother, that was cur'd with *The Sick Man's Salve?*

TRUSTY.

My mother, madam, with the *Salve.*

TRUEWIT.

Then it was *The Sick Woman's Salve.* 105

TRUSTY.

And my father with the *Groats-worth of Wit.* But there was
other means us'd: we had a preacher that would preach folk
asleep still; and so they were prescrib'd to go to church,
by an old woman that was their physician, thrice a week—

95–96. *The Sick Man's Salve*] a tract by Thomas Becon that went through
at least thirteen editions between 1561 and 1607, thus described on the
title page: "Wherein all faithful Christians may learn both how to behave
themselves patiently and thankfully in the time of sickness, and also
vertuously to dispose their temporal goods, and finally to prepare themselves gladly and godly to die."
96–97. *Greene's . . . Wit*] *Greene's Groat's-worth of Wit bought with a Million*
of Repentance (1592) exhorted his fellow dramatists to leave their evil ways.

EPICOENE.

To sleep?   110

TRUSTY.

Yes, forsooth: and every night they read themselves asleep
on those books.

EPICOENE.

Good faith, it stands with great reason. I would I knew
where to procure those books.

MOROSE.

Oh.   115

LA FOOLE.

I can help you with one of 'em, Mistress Morose, the *Groats-
worth of Wit.*

EPICOENE.

But I shall disfurnish you, Sir Amorous; can you spare it?

LA FOOLE.

Oh yes, for a week or so; I'll read it myself to him.

EPICOENE.

No, I must do that sir; that must be my office.   120

MOROSE.

Oh, oh!

EPICOENE.

Sure, he would do well enough if he could sleep.

MOROSE.

No, I should do well enough if you could sleep. Have I no
friend that will make her drunk, or give her a little lau-
danum, or opium?   125

TRUEWIT.

Why, sir, she talks ten times worse in her sleep.

MOROSE.

How!

CLERIMONT.

Do you not know that, sir? Never ceases all night.

TRUEWIT.

And snores like a porcpisce.

MOROSE.

Oh, redeem me, fate; redeem me, fate. For how many 130
causes may a man be divorc'd, nephew?

---

129. *porcpisce*] a porpoise.

DAUPHINE.

    I know not truly, sir.

TRUEWIT.

    Some divine must resolve you in that, sir, or canon lawyer.

MOROSE.

    I will not rest, I will not think of any other hope or comfort,
till I know.   [*Exit with* Dauphine.] 135

CLERIMONT.

    Alas, poor man.

TRUEWIT.

    You'll make him mad indeed, ladies, if you pursue this.

HAUGHTY.

    No, we'll let him breathe now a quarter of an hour or so.

CLERIMONT.

    By my faith, a large truce.

HAUGHTY.

    Is that his keeper that is gone with him?   140

DAW.

    It is his nephew, madam.

LA FOOLE.

    Sir Dauphine Eugenie.

CENTAUR.

    He looks like a very pitiful knight—

DAW.

    As can be. This marriage has put him out of all.

LA FOOLE.

    He has not a penny in his purse, madam—   145

DAW.

    He is ready to cry all this day.

LA FOOLE.

    A very shark, he set me i' the nick t'other night at primero.

TRUEWIT.

    How these swabbers talk!

---

133. *resolve*] i.e., analyze your case of conscience.
147. *shark*] cardsharp.
147. *set . . . nick*] uncertain meaning, possibly "put me down."
147. *primero*] a card game like ombre.
148. *swabbers*] low fellows.

CLERIMONT.

Ay, Otter's wine has swell'd their humors above a spring
tide.   150

HAUGHTY.

Good Morose, let's go in again. I like your couches exceeding well: we'll go lie and talk there.

EPICOENE.

I wait on you, madam.

> [*Exeunt all but* Epicoene, Truewit, Clerimont.]

TRUEWIT.

'Slight, I will have 'em as silent as signs, and their posts
too, ere I ha' done. Do you hear, lady bride? I pray thee 155
now, as thou art a noble wench, continue this discourse of
Dauphine within: but praise him exceedingly. Magnify
him with all the height of affection thou canst (I have some
purpose in't), and but beat off these two rooks, Jack Daw
and his fellow, with any discontentment hither, and I'll 160
honor thee forever.

EPICOENE.

I was about it, here. It anger'd me to the soul to hear 'em
begin to talk so malapert.

TRUEWIT.

Pray thee perform it, and thou winn'st me an idolater to thee
everlasting.   165

EPICOENE.

Will you go in and hear me do it?

TRUEWIT.

No, I'll stay here. Drive 'em out of your company, 'tis all
I ask, which cannot be any way better done than by ex-
tolling Dauphine, whom they have so slighted.

EPICOENE.

I warrant you; you shall expect one of 'em presently.   170

> [*Exit.*]

CLERIMONT.

What a cast of kastrils are these, to hawk after ladies, thus?

TRUEWIT.

Ay, and strike at such an eagle as Dauphine.

---

163. *malapert*] rudely.
171. *cast of kastrils*] pair of cowardly hawks, wind-fuckers. See I.iv.72.

CLERIMONT.

　　He will be mad when we tell him. Here he comes.

[IV.v]   [*Enter*] Dauphine.

CLERIMONT.

　　Oh sir, you are welcome.

TRUEWIT.

　　Where's thine uncle?

DAUPHINE.

　　Run out o' doors in's nightcaps to talk with a casuist about
　　his divorce. It works admirably.

TRUEWIT.

　　Thou wouldst ha' said so and thou hadst been here! The   5
　　ladies have laugh'd at thee most comically since thou went'st
　　Dauphine.

CLERIMONT.

　　And ask'd if thou wert thine uncle's keeper?

TRUEWIT.

　　And the brace of baboons answer'd, "Yes," and said thou
　　wert a pitiful poor fellow and didst live upon posts, and hadst   10
　　nothing but three suits of apparel and some few benevolences
　　that lords ga' thee to fool to 'em and swagger.

DAUPHINE.

　　Let me not live, I'll beat 'em. I'll bind 'em both to grand
　　madam's bedposts, and have 'em baited with monkeys.

TRUEWIT.

　　Thou shalt not need, they shall be beaten to thy hand,   15
　　Dauphine. I have an execution to serve upon 'em, I warrant
　　thee, shall serve: trust my plot.

DAUPHINE.

　　Ay, you have many plots! So you had one to make all the
　　wenches in love with me.

0.1.] Clerimont,　Truewit,　Dauphine, Daw, La Foole. *F1.*

---

　　3. *casuist*] a divine such as William Perkins, whose *Whole Treatise of
Cases of Conscience* (1606) discussed doctrine and practical moral problems.
　　10. *posts*] doing errands.
　　16. *execution*] a legal writ enforcing a judgment.

TRUEWIT.

    Why, if I do not yet afore night, as near as 'tis, and that   20
they do not every one invite thee and be ready to scratch for
thee, take the mortgage of my wit.

CLERIMONT.

    'Fore God, I'll be his witnesse; thou shalt have it, Dau-
phine; thou shalt be his fool forever if thou dost not.

TRUEWIT.

    Agreed. Perhaps 'twill be the better estate. Do you observe   25
this gallery, or rather lobby, indeed? Here are a couple of
studies, at each end one: here will I act such a tragicomedy
between the Guelphs and the Ghibellines, Daw and La
Foole. Which of 'em comes out first will I seize on. You two
shall be the chorus behind the arras, and whip out between   30
the acts and speak. If I do not make 'em keep the peace
for this remnant of the day, if not of the year, I have fail'd
once— I hear Daw coming: hide and do not laugh, for
God's sake.   [*They hide.*]

[Enter Daw.]

DAW.

    Which is the way into the garden, trow?   35

TRUEWIT.

    Oh, Jack Daw! I am glad I have met with you. In good
faith, I must have this matter go no further between you. I
must ha' it taken up.

---

   21. *scratch*] i.e., fight.

   27. *studies*] a technical term of the stage for an enclosed area. Little is
known about the stages of private theaters, but since Morose enters at
IV.vii.1, having found the two swords within, the two studies in this case
were not merely the two doors on either side of the stage.

   27. *tragicomedy*] a new form of serious plays which "want deaths,"
popularized by Beaumont and Fletcher, and acted at Blackfriars Theater
beginning about 1608.

   28. *Guelphs and the Ghibellines*] bloody rivals in power politics of medieval
Italy.

   30. *chorus*] along with the other technical terms such as "catastrophe"
(l. 216), "study," and "tragicomedy," suggests that what follows is a
parody of the play-within-the-play.

   30. *arras*] heavy tapestry that hung at the back of the stage.

   35–317.] The scene may be compared with *Twelfth Night,* III.iv.

DAW.

> What matter, sir? Between whom?

TRUEWIT.

> Come, you disguise it: Sir Amorous and you. If you love me,   40
> Jack, you shall make use of your philosophy now for this
> once and deliver me your sword. This is not the wedding
> the Centaurs were at, though there be a she-one here. The
> bride has entreated me I will see no blood shed at her bridal;
> you saw her whisper me erewhile.   45

DAW.

> As I hope to finish Tacitus, I intend no murder.

TRUEWIT.

> Do you not wait for Sir Amorous?

DAW.

> Not I, by my knighthood.

TRUEWIT.

> And your scholarship too?

DAW.

> And my scholarship too.   50

TRUEWIT.

> Go to, then I return you your sword and ask you mercy; but
> put it not up, for you will be assaulted. I understood that
> you had apprehended it and walk'd here to brave him, and
> that you had held your life contemptible in regard of your
> honor.   55

DAW.

> No, no, no such thing, I assure you. He and I parted now
> as good friends as could be.

TRUEWIT.

> Trust not you to that vizor. I saw him since dinner with
> another face; I have known many men in my time vex'd with
> losses, with deaths and with abuses, but so offended a wight   60
> as Sir Amorous did I never see or read of. For taking away
> his guests, sir, today, that's the cause, and he declares it

---

43. *Centaurs*] "At the marriage of Pirithous . . . with Hippodamia . . . a
drunken Centaur insulted the bride and the wedding ended in a fight"
(H.S.).
46. *Tacitus*] Roman historian, whose works filled a large folio volume.
58. *vizor*] mask.

behind your back with such threat'nings and contempts.
He said to Dauphine, you were the arrant'st ass—

DAW.

Ay, he may say his pleasure.   65

TRUEWIT.

And swears you are so protested a coward that he knows you
will never do him any manly or single right, and therefore he
will take his course.

DAW.

I'll give him any satisfaction, sir—but fighting.

TRUEWIT.

Ay, sir, but who knows what satisfaction he'll take? Blood   70
he thirsts for, and blood he will have: and whereabouts on
you he will have it, who knows but himself?

DAW.

I pray you, Master Truewit, be you a mediator.

TRUEWIT.

Well, sir, conceal yourself then in this study till I return.

                      He puts him up [behind a door].
Nay, you must be content to be lock'd in; for, for mine own   75
reputation I would not have you seen to receive a public disgrace, while I have the matter in managing. Gods so, here
he comes: keep your breath close that he do not hear you
sigh. —In good faith, Sir Amorous, he is not this way; I
pray you be merciful, do not murder him; he is a Christian   80
as good as you; you are arm'd as if you sought a revenge on
all his race. Good Dauphine, get him away from this place.
I never knew a man's choler so high, but he would speak
to his friends, he would hear reason. —Jack Daw. Jack Daw!
Asleep?   85

DAW [*within*].

Is he gone, Master Truewit?

TRUEWIT.

Ay, did you hear him?

DAW.

Oh God, yes.

79. sigh.—] *followed by* he feighnes   there *MS addition F1 (DFo6).*
to speake to Sir Amourous who is not

---

66. *protested*] confessed.

TRUEWIT.

What a quick ear fear has!

DAW [*coming forth*].

But is he so arm'd as you say?   90

TRUEWIT.

Arm'd? Did you ever see a fellow set out to take possession?

DAW.

.   Ay, sir.

TRUEWIT.

That may give you some light to conceive of him; but 'tis
nothing to the principal. Some false brother i' the house has
furnish'd him strangely. Or if it were out o' the house, it   95
was Tom Otter.

DAW.

Indeed, he's a captain and his wife is his kinswoman.

TRUEWIT.

He has got somebody's old two-hand sword, to mow you off
at the knees. And that sword hath spawn'd such a dagger!—
But then he is so hung with pikes, halberds, petronels,   100
calivers, and muskets, that he looks like a justice of peace's
hall: a man of two thousand a year is not cess'd at so many
weapons as he has on. There was never fencer challeng'd
at so many several foils. You would think he meant to
murder all Saint Pulchre's parish. If he could but victual   105
himself for half a year in his breeches, he is sufficiently
arm'd to overrun a country.

100. petronels] peitronels *F1*; pet-
rionels *H.S. conj.*

91. *possession*] "When estates were litigated . . . this was a service of
some danger; and the new owner set forth with his attendants and friends
well armed" (Gifford).

94. *principal*] the original.

95. *furnish'd him strangely*] equipped him marvelously.

100–101. *petronels, calivers*] horse pistols, light muskets.

102. *cess'd*] assessed.

105. *Saint Pulchre's parish*] St. Sepulchre, a populous and rowdy parish
including Newgate prison.

106. *breeches*] "breches . . . slops, or slivings, as now many gentlemen
wear; they are almost capable of [carrying] a bushel of wheat . . . This
absurd, clownish, and unseemly attire, only by custom now is not misliked
but rather approved" (T. Wright, *The Passions of the Minde*, 1601, p. 298,
quoted by H.S.).

DAW.

> Good lord, what means he, sir! I pray you, Master Truewit,
> be you a mediator.

TRUEWIT.

> Well, I'll try if he will be appeas'd with a leg or an arm;   110
> if not, you must die once.

DAW.

> I would be loath to lose my right arm for writing madrigals.

TRUEWIT.

> Why, if he will be satisfied with a thumb or a little finger,
> all's one to me. You must think I'll do my best.

DAW.

> Good sir, do.   115

> *He puts him up again, and then* [Clerimont *and* Dauphine] *come forth.*

CLERIMONT.

> What hast thou done?

TRUEWIT.

> He will let me do nothing, man, he does all afore me, he
> offers his left arm.

CLERIMONT.

> His left wing for a Jack Daw.

DAUPHINE.

> Take it by all means.   120

TRUEWIT.

> How! Maim a man forever for a jest? What a conscience
> hast thou?

DAUPHINE.

> 'Tis no loss to him: he has no employment for his arms but
> to eat spoon meat. Beside, as good maim his body as his
> reputation.   125

TRUEWIT.

> He is a scholar and a wit, and yet he does not think so.
> But he loses no reputation with us, for we all resolv'd him
> an ass before. To your places again.

115.1. *come*] *came F1.*

---

126. *he . . . so*] This may be spoken ironically; Daw pretends that he
does not think himself a scholar; he affects casualness. But "he says it [that
he is a very good scholar] first" (I.ii.71).

CLERIMONT.

    I pray thee, let me be in at the other a little.

TRUEWIT.

    Look, you'll spoil all: these be ever your tricks.   130

CLERIMONT.

    No, but I could hit of some things that thou wilt miss, and
    thou wilt say are good ones.

TRUEWIT.

    I warrant you. I pray forbear, I'll leave it off else.

DAUPHINE.

    Come away, Clerimont.   [*They withdraw again.*]

                    [*Enter* La Foole.]

TRUEWIT.

    Sir Amorous!   135

LA FOOLE.

    Master Truewit.

TRUEWIT.

    Whither were you going?

LA FOOLE.

    Down into the court to make water.

TRUEWIT.

    By no means, sir, you shall rather tempt your breeches.

LA FOOLE.

    Why, sir?   140

TRUEWIT [*opening the other door*].

    Enter here if you love your life.

LA FOOLE.

    Why! why!

TRUEWIT.

    Question till your throat be cut, do: dally till the enraged
    soul find you.

LA FOOLE.

    Who's that?   145

TRUEWIT.

    Daw it is; will you in?

LA FOOLE.

    Ay, ay, I'll in; what's the matter?

TRUEWIT.

    Nay, if he had been cool enough to tell us that, there had

been some hope to atone you, but he seems so implacably
enrag'd.   150

LA FOOLE.

'Slight, let him rage. I'll hide myself.

TRUEWIT.

Do, good sir. But what have you done to him within that
should provoke him thus? You have broke some jest upon
him afore the ladies—

LA FOOLE.

Not I, never in my life broke jest upon any man. The bride 155
was praising Sir Dauphine, and he went away in snuff, and
I followed him, unless he took offence at me in his drink
erewhile, that I would not pledge all the horse full.

TRUEWIT.

By my faith, and that may be, you remember well; but he
walks the round up and down, through every room o' the 160
house, with a towel in his hand, crying "Where's La Foole?
Who saw La Foole?" And when Dauphine and I demanded
the cause, we can force no answer from him but "Oh
revenge, how sweet art thou! I will strangle him in this
towel"—which leads us to conjecture that the main cause 165
of his fury is for bringing your meat today, with a towel
about you, to his discredit.

LA FOOLE.

Like enough. Why, and he be angry for that, I'll stay here
till his anger be blown over.

TRUEWIT.

A good becoming resolution, sir. If you can put it on o' 170
the sudden.

LA FOOLE.

Yes, I can put it on. Or, I'll away into the country presently.

TRUEWIT.

How will you get out o' the house, sir? He knows you are
i' the house, and he'll watch you this se'ennight but he'll
have you. He'll outwait a sergeant for you.   175

155. never] I never *H.S.*

---

156. *snuff*] anger.
172. *presently*] at once.
175. *sergeant*] sheriff's officer who arrested gentlemen for unpaid debts.

LA FOOLE.

Why then I'll stay here.

TRUEWIT.

You must think how to victual yourself in time then.

LA FOOLE.

Why, sweet Master Truewit, will you entreat my cousin
Otter to send me a cold venison pasty, a bottle or two of
wine, and a chamber pot?   180

TRUEWIT.

A stool were better, sir, of Sir A-jax his invention.

LA FOOLE.

Ay, that will be better indeed, and a pallet to lie on.

TRUEWIT.

Oh, I would not advise you to sleep by any means.

LA FOOLE.

Would you not, sir? Why then I will not.

TRUEWIT.

Yet there's another fear—   185

LA FOOLE.

Is there, sir? What is't?

TRUEWIT.

No, he cannot break open this door with his foot, sure.

LA FOOLE.

I'll set my back against it, sir. I have a good back.

TRUEWIT.

But then if he should batter.

LA FOOLE.

Batter! If he dare, I'll have an action of batt'ry against 190
him.

TRUEWIT.

Cast you the worst. He has sent for powder already, and
what he will do with it, no man knows: perhaps blow up the
corner o' the house where he suspects you are. Here he
comes; in quickly. (*He fains as if one were present, to fright the* 195
other, who is run in to hide himself.) I protest, Sir John Daw, he

---

181. *Sir A-jax*] Sir John Harrington's invention of the flushing toilet.
The title of his book explaining it, *The Metamorphosis of Ajax* (1596), puns
on a *jakes* or *jaques*, a privy.
    192. *Cast*] forecast, be prepared for.

is not this way. What will you do? Before God you shall hang
no petard here. I'll die rather. Will you not take my word?
I never knew one but would be satisfied. [*Speaks through the
keyhole.*] Sir Amorous, there's no standing out. He has made 200
a petard of an old brass pot, to force your door. Think upon
some satisfaction or terms to offer him.

LA FOOLE [*within*].

Sir, I'll give him any satisfaction. I dare give any terms.

TRUEWIT.

You'll leave it to me then?

LA FOOLE.

Ay, sir. I'll stand to any conditions.   205

TRUEWIT.

(*He calls forth* Clerimont *and* Dauphine.) How now, what
think you, sirs? Were't not a difficult thing to determine
which of these two fear'd most?

CLERIMONT.

Yes, but this fears the bravest; the other a whiniling
dastard, Jack Daw! But La Foole, a brave heroic coward! 210
And is afraid in a great look and a stout accent. I like him
rarely.

TRUEWIT.

Had it not been pity these two should ha' been conceal'd?

CLERIMONT.

Shall I make a motion?

TRUEWIT.

Briefly. For I must strike while 'tis hot.   215

CLERIMONT.

Shall I go fetch the ladies to the catastrophe?

TRUEWIT.

Umh? Ay, by my troth.

DAUPHINE.

By no mortal means. Let them continue in the state of

209. whiniling] *F1*; whimling *Cunningham conj.*

198. *petard*] bomb.
209. *whiniling*] whindling or whimpering (*OED*).
216. *catastrophe*] denouement; the four parts of a play were protasis,
epitasis, catastasis, and catastrophe.

ignorance and err still: think 'em wits and fine fellows as
they have done. 'Twere sin to reform them.   220

TRUEWIT.

Well, I will have 'em fetch'd, now I think on't, for a
private purpose of mine; do, Clerimont, fetch 'em and discourse to 'em all that's pass'd, and bring 'em into the
gallery here.

DAUPHINE.

This is thy extreme vanity now; thou think'st thou wert 225
undone if every jest thou mak'st were not publish'd.

TRUEWIT.

Thou shalt see how unjust thou art presently. Clerimont,
say it was Dauphine's plot. [*Exit* Clerimont.] Trust me
not if the whole drift be not for thy good. There's a carpet i'
the next room; put it on, with this scarf over thy face and a 230
cushion o' thy head, and be ready when I call Amorous.
Away— [*Exit* Dauphine.] John Daw.

DAW [*entering from his door*].

What good news, sir?

TRUEWIT.

Faith, I have followed and argued with him hard for you.
I told him you were a knight and a scholar, and that you 235
knew fortitude did consist *magis patiendo quam faciendo,*
magis ferendo quam feriendo.

DAW.

It doth so indeed, sir.

TRUEWIT.

And that you would suffer, I told him; so at first he demanded, by my troth, in my conceit, too much.   240

DAW.

What was it, sir?

TRUEWIT.

Your upper lip, and six o' your fore-teeth.

DAW.

'Twas unreasonable.

---

229. *carpet*] tablecloth of thick wool.
236–237. *magis . . . feriendo*] more in suffering than in doing, more in
submitting than in striking.

TRUEWIT.

Nay, I told him plainly, you could not spare 'em all. So
after long argument (*pro et con*, as you know) I brought him 245
down to your two butter-teeth, and them he would have.

DAW.

Oh, did you so? Why, he shall have 'em.

TRUEWIT.

But he shall not, sir, by your leave. The conclusion is this,
sir, because you shall be very good friends hereafter, and
this never to be remember'd or upbraided, besides that he 250
may not boast he has done any such thing to you in his own
person: he is to come here in disguise, give you five kicks in
private, sir, take your sword from you and lock you up in
that study, during pleasure. Which will be but a little while,
we'll get it releas'd presently.   255

DAW.

Five kicks? He shall have six, sir, to be friends.

TRUEWIT.

Believe me, you shall not overshoot yourself to send him
that word by me.

DAW.

Deliver it, sir. He shall have it with all my heart, to be
friends.   260

TRUEWIT.

Friends? Nay, and he should not be so, and heartily too,
upon these terms, he shall have me to enemy while I live.
Come, sir, bear it bravely.

DAW.

Oh God, sir, 'tis nothing.

TRUEWIT.

True. What's six kicks to a man that reads Seneca?   265

DAW.

I have had a hundred, sir.

TRUEWIT.

Sir Amorous.   (Dauphine *comes forth* [*disguised*] *and kicks*

245. *pro et*] *pro & F1.*

---

246. *butter-teeth*] front teeth.
265. *Seneca*] the stoic philosopher.

him.) No speaking one to another, or rehearsing old matters.

DAW.

One, two, three, four, five. I protest, Sir Amorous, you 270 shall have six.

TRUEWIT.

Nay, I told you, you should not talk. Come give him six, and he will needs. [Dauphine *kicks him again.*] Your sword. [*Takes it.*] Now return to your safe custody: you shall presently meet afore the ladies, and be the dearest friends one 275 to another. [*Exit* Daw.] Give me the scarf now, thou shalt beat the other bare-fac'd. Stand by—[Dauphine *withdraws.*] Sir Amorous. [*Unlocks his door.*]

LA FOOLE [*entering*].

What's here? A sword.

TRUEWIT.

I cannot help it, without I should take the quarrel upon 280 myself; here he has sent you his sword—

LA FOOLE.

I'll receive none on't.

TRUEWIT.

And he wills you to fasten it against a wall, and break your head in some few several places against the hilts.

LA FOOLE.

I will not: tell him roundly. I cannot endure to shed my 285 own blood.

TRUEWIT.

Will you not?

LA FOOLE.

No. I'll beat it against a fair flat wall, if that will satisfy him: if not, he shall beat it himself for Amorous.

TRUEWIT.

Why, this is strange starting off when a man undertakes 290 for you! I offered him another condition. Will you stand to that?

LA FOOLE.

Ay, what is't?

272. you, you] *F3*; you *F1*.   277. by—] *H.S.*; by, *F1*.

TRUEWIT.

That you will be beaten in private.

LA FOOLE.

Yes. I am content at the blunt.   295

[*Enter above*, Haughty, Centaur, Mavis, Mrs. Otter, Epicoene, Trusty, Clerimont.]

TRUEWIT.

Then you must submit yourself to be hoodwink'd in this
scarf and be led to him, where he will take your sword from
you and make you bear a blow over the mouth, *gules*, and
tweaks by the nose, *sans nombre*.

LA FOOLE.

I am content. But why must I be blinded?   300

TRUEWIT.

That's for your good, sir; because if he should grow insolent
upon this and publish it hereafter to your disgrace (which I
hope he will not do) you might swear safely and protest he
never beat you, to your knowledge.

LA FOOLE.

Oh, I conceive.   305

TRUEWIT.

I do not doubt but you'll be perfect good friends upon't,
and not dare to utter an ill thought one of another in future.

LA FOOLE.

Not I, as God help me, of him.

TRUEWIT.

Nor he of you, sir. If he should— [*Binds his eyes.*] Come sir.
[*Leads him forward.*] All hid, Sir John.   310

          Dauphine *enters to tweak him.*

LA FOOLE.

Oh, Sir John, Sir John. Oh, o-o-o-o-o-Oh—

295.2. Clerimont] *om. Gifford and
subsequent edns.*

---

295. *at the blunt*] with a sword whose point is blunted.
296. *hoodwink'd*] blindfolded.
298. *gules*] in heraldry, red; he will "bear" the coat of arms of a bloody
mouth, for his courage.
310. *All hid*] a call in playing hide-and-seek (H.S.).

5*   –113–

TRUEWIT.

    Good Sir John, leave tweaking, you'll blow his nose off.
'Tis Sir John's pleasure you should retire into the study. Why
now you are friends. All bitterness between you, I hope, is
buried; you shall come forth by and by, Damon and Pythias 315
upon't, and embrace with all the rankness of friendship that
can be.   [*Exit* La Foole.]
I trust we shall have 'em tamer i' their language hereafter.
Dauphine, I worship thee. God's will, the ladies have
surprised us.   320

[IV.vi]
[*Enter below*] Haughty, Centaur, Mavis, Mrs. Otter, Epicoene, Trusty,
[Clerimont,] *having discover'd part of the past scene above.*

HAUGHTY.

    Centaur, how our judgments were impos'd on by these
adulterate knights!

CENTAUR.

    Nay, madam, Mavis was more deceiv'd than we, 'twas her
commendation utter'd 'em in the college.

MAVIS.

    I commended but their wits, madam, and their braveries. I   5
never look'd toward their valors.

HAUGHTY.

    Sir Dauphine is valiant and a wit too, it seems.

MAVIS.

    And a bravery too.

HAUGHTY.

    Was this his project?

MRS. OTTER.

    So Master Clerimont intimates, madam.   10

0.1.] Haughty, Centaur, Mavis,   Dauphine, Truewit, &c. *F1.*
Mrs. Otter, Epicoene, Trusty,

---

    312. *blow . . . off*] knock it off with a blow.
    315. *Damon and Pythias*] "two philosophers of Pythagoras his sect, in
the league of friendship being each to other most faithful" (Cooper).
[IV.vi]
    4. *utter'd*] introduced.
    5. *braveries*] fine clothes.

HAUGHTY.

Good Morose, when you come to the college, will you bring
him with you? He seems a very perfect gentleman.

EPICOENE.

He is so, madam, believe it.

CENTAUR.

But when will you come, Morose?

EPICOENE.

Three or four days hence, madam, when I have got me a   15
coach and horses.

HAUGHTY.

No, tomorrow, good Morose, Centaur shall send you her
coach.

MAVIS.

Yes faith, do, and bring Sir Dauphine with you.

HAUGHTY.

She has promis'd that, Mavis.   20

MAVIS.

He is a very worthy gentleman in his exteriors, madam.

HAUGHTY.

Ay, he shows he is judicial in his clothes.

CENTAUR.

And yet not so superlatively neat as some, madam, that
have their faces set in a brake!

HAUGHTY.

Ay, and have every hair in form!   25

MAVIS.

That wear purer linen than ourselves, and profess more
neatness than the French hermaphrodite!

EPICOENE.

Ay, ladies, they, what they tell one of us, have told a
thousand and are the only thieves of our fame, that think
to take us with that perfume or with that lace, and laugh   30
at us unconscionably when they have done.

---

24. *set in a brake*] "assume an immovable expression of countenance"
(*OED*).

27. *French hermaphrodite*] King Henry III of France, a notorious trans-
vestite, subject of Thomas Arthus' *Isle des Hermaphrodites* (1605). See
Introduction.

HAUGHTY.

But Sir Dauphine's carelessness becomes him.

CENTAUR.

I could love a man for such a nose!

MAVIS.

Or such a leg!

CENTAUR.

He has an exceeding good eye, madam!   35

MAVIS.

And a very good lock!

CENTAUR.

Good Morose, bring him to my chamber first.

MRS. OTTER.

Please your honors to meet at my house, madam?

TRUEWIT.

See how they eye thee, man! They are taken, I warrant thee.

HAUGHTY [*stepping forward*].

You have unbrac'd our brace of knights here, Master   40
Truewit.

TRUEWIT.

Not I, madam, it was Sir Dauphine's engine; who, if he have
disfurnish'd your ladyship of any guard or service by it,
is able to make the place good again in himself.

HAUGHTY.

There's no suspicion of that, sir.   45

CENTAUR.

God so, Mavis, Haughty is kissing.

MAVIS.

Let us go too and take part.

HAUGHTY.

But I am glad of the fortune (beside the discovery of two
such empty caskets) to gain the knowledge of so rich a mine
of virtue as Sir Dauphine.   50

CENTAUR.   [Centaur *and* Mavis *come forward*.]

We would be all glad to style him of our friendship, and
see him at the college.

---

40. *unbrac'd*] undone, exposed.
42. *engine*] device, contrivance.

MAVIS.

He cannot mix with a sweeter society, I'll prophesy, and I
hope he himself will think so.

DAUPHINE.

I should be rude to imagine otherwise, lady.   55

TRUEWIT.

Did not I tell thee, Dauphine? Why, all their actions are
governed by crude opinion, without reason or cause; they
know not why they do anything; but as they are inform'd,
believe, judge, praise, condemn, love, hate, and in emulation one of another, do all these things alike. Only, they 60
have a natural inclination sways 'em generally to the
worst, when they are left to themselves. But pursue it, now
thou hast 'em.

HAUGHTY.

Shall we go in again, Morose?

EPICOENE.

Yes, madam.   65

CENTAUR.

We'll entreat Sir Dauphine's company.

TRUEWIT.

Stay, good madam, the interview of the two friends, Pylades
and Orestes: I'll fetch 'em out to you straight.

HAUGHTY.

Will you, Master Truewit?

DAUPHINE.

Ay, but noble ladies, do not confess in your countenance 70
or outward bearing to 'em any discovery of their follies, that
we may see how they will bear up again, with what assur-
ance and erection.

HAUGHTY.

We will not, Sir Dauphine.

CENTAUR. MAVIS.

Upon our honors, Sir Dauphine.   75

TRUEWIT [goes to the first door].

Sir Amorous, Sir Amorous. The ladies are here.

---

73. *erection*] high spirits. The sexual pun is appropriate after the ritual
castration.

LA FOOLE [*within*].

Are they?

TRUEWIT.

Yes, but slip out by and by as their backs are turn'd and meet Sir John here, as by chance, when I call you. —Jack Daw [*going to the other door*].   80

DAW [*within*].

What say you, sir?

TRUEWIT.

Whip out behind me suddenly, and no anger i' your looks to your adversary. Now, now.

[*Enter* La Foole *and* Daw.]

LA FOOLE.

Noble Sir John Daw! Where ha' you been?

DAW.

To seek you, Sir Amorous.   85

LA FOOLE.

Me! I honor you.

DAW.

I prevent you, sir.

CLERIMONT.

They have forgot their rapiers!

TRUEWIT.

Oh, they meet in peace, man.

DAUPHINE.

Where's your sword, Sir John?   90

CLERIMONT.

And yours, Sir Amorous?

DAW.

Mine! My boy had it forth to mend the handle, e'en now.

LA FOOLE.

And my gold handle was broke too, and my boy had it forth.

DAUPHINE.

Indeed, sir? How their excuses meet!   95

CLERIMONT.

What a consent there is i' the handles.

TRUEWIT.

Nay, there is so i' the points too, I warrant you.

MRS. OTTER.

Oh me! Madam, he comes again, the madman, away.

[IV.vii]

[*Enter*] Morose: *he had found the two swords drawn within.*

MOROSE.

What make these naked weapons here, gentlemen?

[Ladies, Daw, La Foole *exeunt hastily.*]

TRUEWIT.

Oh, sir! Here hath like to been murder since you went! A
couple of knights fallen out about the bride's favors: we
were fain to take away their weapons; your house had been
begg'd by this time else—   5

MOROSE.

For what?

CLERIMONT.

For manslaughter, sir, as being accessory.

MOROSE.

And for her favors?

TRUEWIT.

Ay, sir, heretofore, not present. Clerimont, carry 'em
their swords now. They have done all the hurt they will do.   10

[*Exit* Clerimont.]

DAUPHINE.

Ha' you spoke with a lawyer, sir?

MOROSE.

Oh no! There is such a noise i' the court that they have
frighted me home with more violence than I went! Such
speaking and counter-speaking, with their several voices
of citations, appellations, allegations, certificates, attach-   15
ments, intergatories, references, convictions, and afflictions
indeed among the doctors and proctors, that the noise here is
silence to't! A kind of calm midnight!

0.1.] Morose, Truewit, Clerimont,
Dauphine. *F1.*

---

5. *begg'd*] "begged for by some courtier in anticipation of the confisca-
tion of Morose's property as that of a criminal" (Bald).

16. *intergatories*] interrogatories.

17. *proctors*] attorneys.

TRUEWIT.

Why, sir, if you would be resolv'd indeed, I can bring you
hither a very sufficient lawyer and a learned divine, that   20
shall inquire into every least scruple for you.

MOROSE.

Can you, Master Truewit?

TRUEWIT.

Yes, and are very sober grave persons, that will dispatch
it in a chamber, with a whisper or two.

MOROSE.

Good sir, shall I hope this benefit from you, and trust myself   25
into your hands?

TRUEWIT.

Alas, sir! Your nephew and I have been asham'd and ofttimes mad since you went, to think how you are abus'd. Go
in, good sir, and lock yourself up till we call you; we'll tell
you more anon, sir.   30

MOROSE.

Do your pleasure with me, gentlemen; I believe in you,
and that deserves no delusion—   [*Exit.*]

TRUEWIT.

You shall find none, sir— but heap'd, heap'd plenty of
vexation.

DAUPHINE.

What wilt thou do now, wit?   35

TRUEWIT.

Recover me hither Otter and the barber if you can, by any
means, presently.

DAUPHINE.

Why? To what purpose?

TRUEWIT.

Oh, I'll make the deepest divine and gravest lawyer out o'
them two, for him—   40

DAUPHINE.

Thou canst not, man; these are waking dreams.

TRUEWIT.

Do not fear me. Clap but a civil gown with a welt o' the one,

33. sir—] *Gifford*; sir: *F1*.

---

36. *Recover*] bring.   42. *civil gown*] robe of a civil lawyer.
42. *welt*] border.

and a canonical cloak with sleeves o' the other, and give
'em a few terms i' their mouths; if there come not forth as
able a doctor and complete a parson for this turn as may be   45
wish'd, trust not my election. And I hope, without wronging
the dignity of either profession, since they are but persons
put on, and for mirth's sake, to torment him. The barber
smatters Latin, I remember.

DAUPHINE.
Yes, and Otter too.   50

TRUEWIT.
Well then, if I make 'em not wrangle out this case to his
no comfort, let me be thought a Jack Daw or La Foole or
anything worse. Go you to your ladies, but first send for
them.

DAUPHINE.
I will.   [*Exeunt.*] 55

[V.i]   [*Enter*] La Foole, Clerimont, Daw.

LA FOOLE.
Where had you our swords, Master Clerimont?

CLERIMONT.
Why, Dauphine took 'em from the madman.

LA FOOLE.
And he took 'em from our boys, I warrant you.

CLERIMONT.
Very like, sir.

LA FOOLE.
Thank you, good Master Clerimont. Sir John Daw and I are   5
both beholden to you.

CLERIMONT.
Would I knew how to make you so, gentlemen.

DAW.
Sir Amorous and I are your servants, sir.

[*Enter* Mavis.]

MAVIS.
Gentlemen, have any of you a pen and ink? I would fain
write out a riddle in Italian for Sir Dauphine to translate.   10

0.1.] La Foole, Clerimont, Daw,
Mavis. *F1.*

CLERIMONT.

Not I, in troth, lady, I am no scrivener.

DAW.

I can furnish you, I think, lady.

CLERIMONT.

He has it in the haft of a knife, I believe.

LA FOOLE.

No, he has his box of instruments.

CLERIMONT.

Like a surgeon!   15

LA FOOLE.

For the mathematics: his squire, his compasses, his brass
pens, and black lead, to draw maps of every place and
person where he comes.

CLERIMONT.

How, maps of persons!

LA FOOLE.

Yes, sir, of Nomentack, when he was here, and of the   20
Prince of Moldavia, and of his mistress, Mistress Epicoene.

CLERIMONT.

Away! He has not found out her latitude, I hope.

LA FOOLE.

You are a pleasant gentleman, sir.   [*Exit* Mavis.]

CLERIMONT.

Faith, now we are in private, let's wanton it a little and
talk waggishly. —Sir John, I am telling Sir Amorous here   25
that you two govern the ladies; where'er you come, you
carry the feminine gender afore you.

DAW.

They shall rather carry us afore them if they will, sir.

12. lady.] *followed by: Exeunt* Daw   21.] Epicoene] *followed by: Re-*
and Mavis. *Gifford.*   *enter* Daw. *Gifford.*

13. *haft of a knife*] not incredible, for Thomas Hobbes carried pen and
ink in the handle of his walking stick (Aubrey, II, 334).
16. *squire*] square.
20. *Nomentack*] Namontack, adviser of Powhatan, brought as a hostage
to England 1608–1609 (Capt. John Smith, *Works*, ed. Arber, 1884, pp.
102, 405, 517, 608).
21. *Prince of Moldavia*] See Introduction.

CLERIMONT.

Nay, I believe that they do, withal; but that you are the
prime men in their affections, and direct all their actions—   30

DAW.

Not I; Sir Amorous is.

LA FOOLE.

I protest, Sir John is.

DAW.

As I hope to rise i' the state, Sir Amorous, you ha' the
person.

LA FOOLE.

Sir John, you ha' the person and the discourse too.   35

DAW.

Not I, sir. I have no discourse—and then you have activity
beside.

LA FOOLE.

I protest, Sir John, you come as high from Tripoly as I do
every whit, and lift as many join'd stools and leap over 'em,
if you would use it—   40

CLERIMONT.

Well, agree on't together, knights, for between you, you
divide the kingdom or commonwealth of ladies' affections. I
see it and can perceive a little how they observe you and fear
you, indeed. You could tell strange stories, my masters, if
you would, I know.   45

DAW.

Faith, we have seen somewhat, sir.

LA FOOLE.

That we have: velvet petticoats and wrought smocks or so.

DAW.

Ay, and—

CLERIMONT.

Nay, out with it, Sir John; do not envy your friend the
pleasure of hearing, when you have had the delight of   50
tasting.

---

38. *come ... Tripoly*] "To vault and tumble with activity. It was, I
believe, first applied to the tricks of an ape or monkey, which might be
supposed to come from that part of the world" (Nares).

47. *velvet petticoats*] worn by courtly ladies and high-class prostitutes.

DAW.

Why—a—do you speak, Sir Amorous.

LA FOOLE.

No, do you, Sir John Daw.

DAW.

I' faith, you shall.

LA FOOLE.

I' faith, you shall.   55

DAW.

Why, we have been—

LA FOOLE.

In The Great Bed at Ware together in our time. On, Sir
John.

DAW.

Nay, do you, Sir Amorous.

CLERIMONT.

And these ladies with you, knights?   60

LA FOOLE.

No, excuse us, sir.

DAW.

We must not wound reputation.

LA FOOLE.

No matter; they were these or others. Our bath cost us
fifteen pound when we came home.

CLERIMONT.

Do you hear, Sir John, you shall tell me but one thing   65
truly, as you love me.

DAW.

If I can, I will, sir.

CLERIMONT.

You lay in the same house with the bride here?

DAW.

Yes, and convers'd with her hourly, sir.

CLERIMONT.

And what humor is she of? Is she coming and open, free?   70

---

57. *Great . . . Ware*] a bed eleven feet square, formerly at the Saracen's
Head, Ware, now in the Victoria and Albert Museum, supposed to sleep
twelve people.

DAW.

Oh, exceeding open, sir. I was her servant, and Sir Amorous
was to be.

CLERIMONT.

Come, you have both had favors from her? I know and
have heard so much.

DAW.

Oh, no sir.   75

LA FOOLE.

You shall excuse us, sir: we must not wound reputation.

CLERIMONT.

Tut, she is married now, and you cannot hurt her with any
report, and therefore speak plainly: how many times, i'
faith? Which of you led first? Ha?

LA FOOLE.

Sir John had her maidenhead, indeed.   80

DAW.

Oh, it pleases him to say so, sir, but Sir Amorous knows
what's what as well.

CLERIMONT.

Dost thou i' faith, Amorous?

LA FOOLE.

In a manner, sir.

CLERIMONT.

Why, I commend you lads. Little knows Don Bridegroom   85
of this. Nor shall he, for me.

DAW.

Hang him, mad ox.

CLERIMONT.

Speak softly; here comes his nephew with the Lady Haughty.
He'll get the ladies from you, sirs, if you look not to him in
time.   90

LA FOOLE.

Why, if he do, we'll fetch 'em home again, I warrant you.

[*Exeunt.*]

91.1. *Exeunt*] *Exit with* Daw. Cler.
walks aside. Gifford.

91.1.] Gifford and all subsequent editors have allowed Clerimont to
remain on stage, although he does not speak again until V.ii.43. He
probably should go off with Daw and La Foole to pump more facts from
them of "times and circumstances".

[V.ii]   [*Enter*] Haughty, Dauphine.

HAUGHTY.

I assure you, Sir Dauphine, it is the price and estimation
of your virtue only that hath embark'd me to this adventure,
and I could not but make out to tell you so; nor can I
repent me of the act, since it is always an argument of some
virtue in ourselves that we love and affect it so in others.   5

DAUPHINE.

Your ladyship sets too high a price on my weakness.

HAUGHTY.

Sir, I can distinguish gems from pebbles—

DAUPHINE [*aside*].

Are you so skilful in stones?

HAUGHTY.

And howsoever I may suffer in such a judgment as yours,
by admitting equality of rank or society with Centaur or   10
Mavis—

DAUPHINE.

You do not, madam; I perceive they are your mere foils.

HAUGHTY.

Then are you a friend to truth, sir. It makes me love you
the more. It is not the outward but the inward man that I
affect. They are not apprehensive of an eminent perfection,   15
but love flat and dully.

CENTAUR [*within*].

Where are you, my lady Haughty?

HAUGHTY.

I come presently, Centaur. —My chamber, sir, my page
shall show you; and Trusty, my woman, shall be ever awake
for you; you need not fear to communicate anything with   20
her, for she is a Fidelia. I pray you wear this jewel for my
sake, Sir Dauphine.

[*Enter* Centaur.]

Where's Mavis, Centaur?

CENTAUR.

Within, madam, a-writing. I'll follow you presently. I'll
but speak a word with Sir Dauphine.   [*Exit* Haughty.]   25

0.1.] Haughty, Dauphine, Centaur,   8. Are ... stones?] (Are ... stones?)
Mavis, Clerimont. *F1.*   *F1.*

DAUPHINE.

With me, madam?

CENTAUR.

Good Sir Dauphine, do not trust Haughty, nor make any
credit to her, whatever you do besides. Sir Dauphine, I give
you this caution, she is a perfect courtier and loves nobody
but for her uses, and for her uses she loves all. Besides, her 30
physicians give her out to be none o' the clearest; whether
she pay 'em or no, heav'n knows; and she's above fifty too,
and pargets! See her in a forenoon. Here comes Mavis, a
worse face than she! You would not like this by candlelight. If you'll come to my chamber one o' these mornings 35
early, or late in an evening, I'll tell you more.

[*Enter* Mavis.]

Where's Haughty, Mavis?

MAVIS.

Within, Centaur.

CENTAUR.

What ha' you there?

MAVIS.

An Italian riddle for Sir Dauphine. [*Aside.*] You shall not 40
see it i' faith, Centaur. —Good Sir Dauphine, solve it for
me. I'll call for it anon.   [*Exeunt* Centaur, Mavis.]

[*Enter* Clerimont.]

CLERIMONT.

How now, Dauphine? How dost thou quit thyself of these
females?

DAUPHINE.

'Slight, they haunt me like fairies, and give me jewels here; 45
I cannot be rid of 'em.

CLERIMONT.

Oh, you must not tell though.

40–41. You . . . Centaur.—] (You
. . . Centaur.) *F1.*

27–28. *make any credit to*] set any store by (*OED*).
33. *pargets*] i.e., plasters herself with make-up.
47. *not tell*] "To confide in any one about a fairy's gift rendered it void"
(Henry).

DAUPHINE.

 Mass, I forgot that: I was never so assaulted. One loves
for virtue, and bribes me with this. Another loves me with
caution, and so would possess me. A third brings me a riddle 50
here; and all are jealous and rail each at other.

CLERIMONT.

 A riddle? Pray le' me see't?   *He reads the paper.*
"SIR DAUPHINE,

 I chose this way of intimation for privacy. The ladies here,
I know, have both hope and purpose to make a collegiate 55
and servant of you. If I might be so honor'd as to appear
at any end of so noble a work, I would enter into a fame of
taking physic tomorrow and continue it four or five days or
longer, for your visitation.

      MAVIS."   60
By my faith, a subtle one! Call you this a riddle? What's
their plain dealing, trow?

DAUPHINE.

 We lack Truewit to tell us that.

CLERIMONT.

 We lack him for somewhat else too: his knights *reformados*
are wound up as high and insolent as ever they were. 65

DAUPHINE.

 You jest.

CLERIMONT.

 No drunkards, either with wine or vanity, ever confess'd such
stories of themselves. I would not give a fly's leg in balance
against all the women's reputations here, if they could be
but thought to speak truth; and for the bride, they have 70
made their affidavit against her directly—

DAUPHINE.

 What, that they have lien with her?

CLERIMONT.

 Yes, and tell times and circumstances, with the cause why
and the place where. I had almost brought 'em to affirm
that they had done it today. 75

---

57. *fame*] rumor.
64. *reformados*] disbanded soldiers.

DAUPHINE.

Not both of 'em.

CLERIMONT.

Yes, faith; with a sooth or two more I had effected it. They
would ha' set it down under their hands.

DAUPHINE.

Why, they will be our sport, I see, still! whether we will or
no.   80

[V.iii]   [*Enter*] Truewit.

TRUEWIT.

Oh, are you here? Come, Dauphine. Go, call your uncle
presently. I have fitted my divine and my canonist, dyed
their beards and all; the knaves do not know themselves,
they are so exalted and alter'd. Preferment changes any
man. Thou shalt keep one door and I another, and then   5
Clerimont in the midst, that he may have no means of
escape from their caviling when they grow hot once. And
then the women (as I have given the bride her instructions)
to break in upon him i' the *l'envoy*. Oh, 'twill be full and
twanging! Away, fetch him.   [*Exit* Dauphine.]   10

[*Enter* Otter *disguised as a divine,* Cutbeard *as a canon lawyer.*]

Come, master doctor and master parson, look to your parts
now and discharge 'em bravely; you are well set forth, perform it as well. If you chance to be out, do not confess it with
standing still or humming or gaping one at another, but go
on and talk aloud and eagerly, use vehement action, and   15
only remember your terms and you are safe. Let the
matter go where it will: you have many will do so. But at
first be very solemn and grave like your garments, though
you loose yourselves after and skip out like a brace of

0.1.] Truewit, Morose, Otter, Cutbeard, Clerimont, Dauphine. *F1.*

---

77. *a sooth or two*] a few more exclamations by me, "in sooth," i.e.,
indeed.
[V.iii]
  9. *l'envoy*] end.
  10. *twanging*] first rate.
  15. *action*] movement of the arms.

jugglers on a table. Here he comes! Set your faces, and look   20
superciliously while I present you.

[*Enter* Dauphine *and* Morose.]

MOROSE.

Are these the two learned men?

TRUEWIT.

Yes, sir; please you salute 'em?

MOROSE.

Salute 'em? I had rather do anything than wear out time
so unfruitfully, sir. I wonder how these common forms, as   25
"God save you" and "You are welcome," are come to be a
habit in our lives! Or "I am glad to see you!" when I
cannot see what the profit can be of these words, so long as
it is no whit better with him whose affairs are sad and
grievous, that he hears this salutation.   30

TRUEWIT.

'Tis true, sir, we'll go to the matter then. Gentlemen, master
doctor and master parson, I have acquainted you sufficiently
with the business for which you are come hither. And you
are not now to inform yourselves in the state of the question,
I know. This is the gentleman who expects your resolution,   35
and therefore, when you please, begin.

OTTER.

Please you, master doctor.

CUTBEARD.

Please you, good master parson.

OTTER.

I would hear the canon law speak first.

CUTBEARD.

It must give place to positive divinity, sir.   40

MOROSE.

Nay, good gentlemen, do not throw me into circumstances.
Let your comforts arrive quickly at me, those that are. Be
swift in affording me my peace, if so I shall hope any. I love
not your disputations or your court tumults. And that it be
not strange to you, I will tell you. My father, in my edu-   45

---

40. *positive divinity*] practical laws for conduct, set forth in scripture or
by the church.

cation, was wont to advise me that I should always collect
and contain my mind, not suff'ring it to flow loosely, that
I should look to what things were necessary to the carriage
of my life, and what not, embracing the one and eschewing
the other. In short, that I should endear myself to rest and   50
avoid turmoil, which now is grown to be another nature
to me. So that I come not to your public pleadings or your
places of noise, not that I neglect those things that make for
the dignity of the commonwealth, but for the mere avoiding
of clamors and impertinencies of orators that know not   55
how to be silent. And for the cause of noise am I now a
suitor to you. You do not know in what a misery I have
been exercis'd this day, what a torrent of evil! My very
house turns round with the tumult! I dwell in a windmill!
The perpetual motion is here, and not at Eltham.   60

TRUEWIT.

Well, good master doctor, will you break the ice? Master
parson will wade after.

CUTBEARD.

Sir, though unworthy and the weaker, I will presume.

OTTER.

'Tis no presumption, *domine* doctor.

MOROSE.

Yet again!   65

CUTBEARD.

Your question is, for how many causes a man may have
divortium legitimum, a lawful divorce. First, you must under-
stand the nature of the word divorce, *à divertendo*—

MOROSE.

No excursions upon words, good doctor; to the question
briefly.   70

CUTBEARD.

I answer then, the canon law affords divorce but in few

55. impertinencies] *F1 (corr.)*; pertinencies *F1 (uncorr.)*.

---

60. *Eltham*] southeast of London at the royal park, where Cornelis
Drebbel showed his "wittie invention of an artificial perpetual motion"
(title page of his *Dialogue Philosophical*, 1612).
64. *domine*] master.
68. *à divertendo*] derived from "separating."

cases, and the principal is in the common case, the adulterous case. But there are *duodecim impedimenta*, twelve impediments (as we call 'em) all which do not *dirimere contractum*, but *irritum reddere matrimonium*, as we say in the   75 canon law, not take away the bond but cause a nullity therein.

MOROSE.

I understood you before; good sir, avoid your impertinency of translation.

OTTER.

He cannot open this too much, sir, by your favor.   80

MOROSE.

Yet more!

TRUEWIT.

Oh, you must give the learned men leave, sir. To your impediments, master doctor.

CUTBEARD.

The first is *impedimentum erroris*.

OTTER.

Of which there are several species.   85

CUTBEARD.

Ay, as *error personae*.

OTTER.

If you contract yourself to one person, thinking her another.

CUTBEARD.

Then, *error fortunae*.

OTTER.

If she be a beggar, and you thought her rich.

CUTBEARD.

Then, *error qualitatis*.   90

OTTER.

If she prove stubborn or headstrong, that you thought obedient.

73–74. *twelve impediments*] These twelve hindrances are listed in this order by Thomas Aquinas (Henry). The Earl of Essex's divorce in 1613, where bishops Neal and Andrews were "the very counterparts of Otter and Cutbeard," bears a striking resemblance to this burlesque (Gifford). Since Essex's divorce was granted upon the twelfth impediment, one wonders if Jonson revised the play between 1609 and 1616.

80. *open*] clarify.

MOROSE.

How? Is that, sir, a lawful impediment? One at once, I
pray you, gentlemen.

OTTER.

Ay, *ante copulam*, but not *post copulam*, sir.   95

CUTBEARD.

Master parson says right. *Nec post nuptiarum benedictionem*. It
doth indeed but *irrita reddere sponsalia*, annul the contract;
after marriage it is of no obstancy.

TRUEWIT.

Alas, sir, what a hope are we fall'n from by this time!

CUTBEARD.

The next is *conditio*: if you thought her freeborn and she 100
prove a bond-woman, there is impediment of estate and
condition.

OTTER.

Ay, but master doctor, those servitudes are *sublatae* now
among us Christians.

CUTBEARD.

By your favor, master parson—   105

OTTER.

You shall give me leave, master doctor.

MOROSE.

Nay, gentlemen, quarrel not in that question; it concerns
not my case: pass to the third.

CUTBEARD.

Well then, the third is *votum*. If either party have made a
vow of chastity. But that practice, as master parson said of 110
the other, is taken away among us, thanks be to discipline.
The fourth is *cognatio*: if the persons be of kin, within the
degrees.

OTTER.

Ay, do you know what the degrees are, sir?

---

96. *Nec . . . benedictionem*] And not after the sacrament of marriage.
97. *contract*] the betrothal.
98. *obstancy*] juridical opposition (*OED*).
103. *sublatae*] abolished.
111. *discipline*] teaching of the reformed churches.

MOROSE.

No, nor I care not, sir; they offer me no comfort in the 115
question, I am sure.

CUTBEARD.

But there is a branch of this impediment may, which is
cognatio spiritualis. If you were her godfather, sir, then the
marriage is incestuous.

OTTER.

That comment is absurd and superstitious, master doctor. I 120
cannot endure it. Are we not all brothers and sisters, and as
much akin in that as godfathers and goddaughters?

MOROSE.

Oh me! To end the controversy, I never was a godfather, I
never was a godfather in my life, sir. Pass to the next.

CUTBEARD.

The fifth is *crimen adulterii*: the known case. The sixth, *cultus* 125
disparitas, difference of religion; have you ever examin'd her
what religion she is of?

MOROSE.

No, I would rather she were of none, than be put to the
trouble of it!

OTTER.

You may have it done for you, sir.   130

MOROSE.

By no means, good sir; on to the rest; shall you ever come to
an end, think you?

TRUEWIT.

Yes, he has done half, sir. —On to the rest. —Be patient and
expect, sir.

CUTBEARD.

The seventh is *vis*: if it were upon compulsion or force.   135

MOROSE.

Oh no, it was too voluntary, mine; too voluntary.

CUTBEARD.

The eighth is *ordo*: if ever she have taken holy orders.

OTTER.

That's superstitious too.

133. —On . . . rest.—] (On . . . rest.)
F1.

MOROSE.

No matter, master parson: would she would go into a
nunnery yet.   140

CUTBEARD.

The ninth is *ligamen*: if you were bound, sir, to any other
before.

MOROSE.

I thrust myself too soon into these fetters.

CUTBEARD.

The tenth is *publica honestas*: which is *inchoata quaedam
affinitas*.   145

OTTER.

Ay, or *affinitas orta ex sponsalibus*, and is but *leve impedimentum*.

MOROSE.

I feel no air of comfort blowing to me in all this.

CUTBEARD.

The eleventh is *affinitas ex fornicatione*.

OTTER.

Which is no less *vera affinitas* than the other, master doctor.

CUTBEARD.

True, *quae oritur ex legitimo matrimonio*.   150

OTTER.

You say right, venerable doctor. And *nascitur ex eo, quod per
conjugium duae personae efficiuntur una caro*—

MOROSE.

Heyday, now they begin.

153. S.P. MOROSE.] *F1*; True. *Gifford*.

---

144. *publica honestas*] "previous espousal, or previous marriage which has
not been consummated" (Henry).

144–145. *inchoata quaedam affinitas*] some uncompleted relationship by
marriage, as distinct from blood relationship.

146. *affinitas . . . sponsalibus*] relationship arising out of a betrothal.

146. *leve impedimentum*] slight impediment.

148. *affinitas ex fornicatione*] relationship from fornication; i.e., with a near
relative of one's betrothed.

149. *vera affinitas*] true relationship.

150. *quae . . . matrimonio*] which arises from legal marriage.

151–152. *nascitur . . . caro*—] it proceeds from this, that through physical
union in marriage two people are made one flesh.

CUTBEARD.

I conceive you, master parson. *Ita per fornicationem aeque
est verus pater, qui sic generat—*   155

OTTER.

Et vere filius qui sic generatur—

MOROSE.

What's all this to me?

CLERIMONT.

Now it grows warm.

CUTBEARD.

The twelfth and last is *si forte coire nequibis.*

OTTER.

Ay, that is *impedimentum gravissimum.* It doth utterly annul 160
and annihilate, that. If you have *manifestam frigiditatem,*
you are well, sir.

TRUEWIT.

Why, there is comfort come at length, sir. Confess yourself
but a man unable, and she will sue to be divorc'd first.

OTTER.

Ay, or if there be *morbus perpetuus et insanabilis,* as paralysis, 165
elephantiasis, or so—

DAUPHINE.

Oh, but *frigiditas* is the fairer way, gentlemen.

OTTER.

You say troth, sir, and as it is in the canon, master doctor.

CUTBEARD.

I conceive you, sir.

CLERIMONT.

Before he speaks.   170

OTTER.

That a boy or child under years is not fit for marriage
because he cannot *reddere debitum.* So your *omnipotentes—*

154–155. *Ita ... generat—*] So in respect to fornication he is equally a
true father who thus begets.

156. *Et ... generatur—*] And a true son who is thus begotten.

159. *si ... nequibis*] if by chance you be unable to copulate.

160. *impedimentum gravissimum*] a very serious impediment.

161. *manifestam frigiditatem*] evident frigidity.

165. *morbus ... insanabilis*] a continual and incurable disorder.

172. *reddere debitum*] fulfill the obligation; literally, pay the debt.

TRUEWIT.

Your *impotentes*, you whoreson lobster.

OTTER.

Your *impotentes*, I should say, are *minime apti ad contrahenda matrimonium*.   175

TRUEWIT.

Matrimonium? We shall have most unmatrimonial Latin with you: *matrimonia* and be hang'd.

DAUPHINE.

You put 'em out, man.

CUTBEARD.

But then there will arise a doubt, master parson, in our case, *post matrimonium*, that *frigiditate praeditus*—do you conceive 180 me, sir?

OTTER.

Very well, sir.

CUTBEARD.

Who cannot *uti uxore pro uxore*, may *habere eam pro sorore*.

OTTER.

Absurd, absurd, absurd, and merely apostatical.

CUTBEARD.

You shall pardon me, master parson, I can prove it.   185

OTTER.

You can prove a will, master doctor, you can prove nothing else. Does not the verse of your own canon say, *Haec socianda vetant conubia, facta retractant—*

CUTBEARD.

I grant you, but how do they *retractare*, master parson?

MOROSE.

(Oh, this was it, I fear'd.)   190

OTTER.

In aeternum, sir.

174–175. *minime . . . matrimonium*] least fit for contracting marriage.
180. *frigiditate praeditus*] one afflicted with frigidity.
183. *uti . . . sorore*] use a wife as a wife, may keep her as a sister.
187–188. *Haec . . . retractant*] These things forbid joining in marriage, and having made a marriage revoke it. A quotation from Aquinas, after he has listed the twelve impediments (Henry).
191. *In aeternum*] to all eternity, forever.

CUTBEARD.

That's false in divinity, by your favor.

OTTER.

'Tis false in humanity to say so. Is he not *prorsus inutilis ad thorum?* Can he *praestare fidem datam?* I would fain know.

CUTBEARD.

Yes, how if he do *convalere?*   195

OTTER.

He cannot *convalere,* it is impossible.

TRUEWIT.

Nay, good sir, attend the learned men; they'll think you neglect 'em else.

CUTBEARD.

Or, if he do *simulare* himself *frigidum, odio uxoris,* or so?

OTTER.

I say he is *adulter manifestus* then.   200

DAUPHINE.

(They dispute it very learnedly, i' faith.)

OTTER.

And *prostitutor uxoris,* and this is positive.

MOROSE.

Good sir, let me escape.

TRUEWIT.

You will not do me that wrong, sir?

OTTER.

And therefore if he be *manifeste frigidus,* sir—   205

CUTBEARD.

Ay, if he be *manifeste frigidus,* I grant you—

OTTER.

Why, that was my conclusion.

CUTBEARD.

And mine too.

193–194. *prorsus . . . thorum*] completely useless in bed. A pun on *thorus,* bull.
194. *praestare fidem datam*] fulfill the promise given.
195. *convalere*] recover.
199. *simulare . . . uxoris*] falsely represent himself to be frigid, on account of hatred for his wife.
200. *adulter manifestus*] manifest adulterer.
202. *prostitutor uxoris*] a prostitutor of his wife.

TRUEWIT.

Nay, hear the conclusion, sir.

OTTER.

Then *frigiditatis causa*—   210

CUTBEARD.

Yes, *causa frigiditatis*—

MOROSE.

Oh, mine ears!

OTTER.

She may have *libellum divortii* against you.

CUTBEARD.

Ay, *divortii libellum* she will sure have.

MOROSE.

Good echoes, forbear.   215

OTTER.

If you confess it.

CUTBEARD.

Which I would do, sir—

MOROSE.

I will do anything—

OTTER.

And clear myself *in foro conscientiae*—

CUTBEARD.

Because you want indeed—   220

MOROSE.

Yet more?

OTTER.

Exercendi potestate.

[V.iv.]

[*Enter*] Epicoene, Haughty, Centaur, Mavis, Mrs. Otter, Daw, La
Foole.

EPICOENE.

I will not endure it any longer. Ladies, I beseech you help

0.1–0.2.] Epicoene, Morose,   Clerimont, La Foole, Otter, Cut-
Haughty, Centaur, Mavis, Mrs.   beard. *F1.*
Otter, Daw, Truewit, Dauphine,

---

213. *libellum divortii*] bill of divorce.
219. *in foro conscientiae*] at the bar of conscience.
222. *Exercendi potestate*] the power of raising [his sword] (Cooper).

me. This is such a wrong as never was offer'd to poor bride
before. Upon her marriage day, to have her husband con-
spire against her, and a couple of mercenary companions
to be brought in for form's sake to persuade a separation!   5
If you had blood or virtue in you, gentlemen, you would not
suffer such earwigs about a husband, or scorpions to creep
between man and wife—

MOROSE.

Oh, the variety and changes of my torment!

HAUGHTY.

Let 'em be cudgell'd out of doors by our grooms.   10

CENTAUR.

I'll lend you my footman.

MAVIS.

We'll have our men blanket 'em i' the hall.

MRS. OTTER.

As there was one at our house, madam, for peeping in at
the door.

DAW.

Content, i' faith.   15

TRUEWIT.

Stay, ladies and gentlemen, you'll hear before you proceed?

MAVIS.

I'ld ha' the bridegroom blanketed too.

CENTAUR.

Begin with him first.

HAUGHTY.

Yes, by my troth.

MOROSE.

Oh, mankind generation!   20

DAUPHINE.

Ladies, for my sake forbear.

HAUGHTY.

Yes, for Sir Dauphine's sake.

---

7. *earwigs*] prying informers, who "creep into your ears" (George
Chapman, *Monsieur D'Olive*, 1606, sig. H3, cited by H.S.).

12. *blanket*] toss in a blanket.

20. *mankind*] "Not 'masculine' as . . . 'mankind Maid' in [Jonson's] *For.*
x. 13, but a separate word connected with 'mankeen' and meaning 'in-
furiated,' 'mad'" (H.S.).

CENTAUR.

He shall command us.

LA FOOLE.

He is as fine a gentleman of his inches, madam, as any is
about the town, and wears as good colors when he list.   25

TRUEWIT.

Be brief, sir, and confess your infirmity, she'll be afire to be
quit of you; if she but hear that nam'd once, you shall not
entreat her to stay. She'll fly you like one that had the marks
upon him.

MOROSE.

Ladies, I must crave all your pardons—   30

TRUEWIT.

Silence, ladies.

MOROSE.

For a wrong I have done to your whole sex in marrying this
fair and virtuous gentlewoman—

CLERIMONT.

Hear him, good ladies.

MOROSE.

Being guilty of an infirmity which, before I conferr'd with   35
these learned men, I thought I might have conceal'd—

TRUEWIT.

But now being better inform'd in his conscience by them,
he is to declare it and give satisfaction by asking your
public forgiveness.

MOROSE.

I am no man, ladies.   40

ALL.

How!

MOROSE.

Utterly unabled in nature, by reason of frigidity, to perform
the duties or any the least office of a husband.

MAVIS.

Now, out upon him, prodigious creature!

---

24. *gentleman of his inches*] "a notable fellow" (*OED*).
28. *marks*] signs of the plague.

CENTAUR.

> Bridegroom uncarnate.   45

HAUGHTY.

> And would you offer it to a young gentlewoman?

MRS. OTTER.

> A lady of her longings?

EPICOENE.

> Tut, a device, a device, this, it smells rankly, ladies. A mere
> comment of his own.

TRUEWIT.

> Why, if you suspect that, ladies, you may have him search'd.   50

DAW.

> As the custom is, by a jury of physicians.

LA FOOLE.

> Yes, faith, 'twill be brave.

MOROSE.

> Oh me, must I undergo that!

MRS. OTTER.

> No, let women search him, madam: we can do it ourselves.

MOROSE.

> Out on me, worse!   55

EPICOENE.

> No, ladies, you shall not need, I'll take him with all his
> faults.

MOROSE.

> Worst of all!

CLERIMONT.

> Why, then 'tis no divorce, doctor, if she consent not?

CUTBEARD.

> No, if the man be *frigidus*, it is *de parte uxoris* that we grant   60
> *libellum divortii* in the law.

OTTER.

> Ay, it is the same in theology.

MOROSE.

> Worse, worse than worst!

---

45. *uncarnate*] a nonce word, by humorous analogy with "incarnate,"
without flesh and blood.
49. *comment*] "sometimes . . . taken for a lie or fained tale" (Bullokar,
An English Expositor, 1616, cited in *OED*).

TRUEWIT.

    Nay, sir, be not utterly dishearten'd; we have yet a small
relic of hope left, as near as our comfort is blown out. 65
Clerimont, produce your brace of knights. What was that,
master parson, you told me *in errore qualitatis*, e'en now?—
Dauphine, whisper the bride that she carry it as if she were
guilty and asham'd.

OTTER.

    Marry, sir, *in errore qualitatis* (which master doctor did for- 70
bear to urge) if she be found *corrupta*, that is, vitiated or
broken up, that was *pro virgine desponsa*, espous'd for a
maid—

MOROSE.

    What then, sir?

OTTER.

    It doth *dirimere contractum* and *irritum reddere* too.   75

TRUEWIT.

    If this be true, we are happy again, sir, once more. Here
are an honorable brace of knights that shall affirm so much.

DAW.

    Pardon us, good Master Clerimont.

LA FOOLE.

    You shall excuse us, Master Clerimont.

CLERIMONT.

    Nay, you must make it good now, knights; there is no 80
remedy; I'll eat no words for you nor no men: you know
you spoke it to me?

DAW.

    Is this gentleman-like, sir?

TRUEWIT [*aside to* Daw].

    Jack Daw, he's worse than Sir Amorous, fiercer a great deal.
[*Aside to* La Foole.]   Sir Amorous, beware, there be ten 85
Daws in this Clerimont.

LA FOOLE.

    I'll confess it, sir.

DAW.

    Will you, Sir Amorous? Will you wound reputation?

---

   75. *dirimere . . . reddere*] cancel the contract and render it null and
void.

LA FOOLE.

  I am resolv'd.

TRUEWIT.

  So should you be too, Jack Daw: what should keep you off?   90
  She is but a woman, and in disgrace. He'll be glad on't.

DAW.

  Will he? I thought he would ha' been angry.

CLERIMONT.

  You will dispatch, knights, it must be done, i' faith.

TRUEWIT.

  Why, an' it must it shall, sir, they say. They'll ne'er go back.
  Do not tempt his patience.   95

DAW.

  It is true indeed, sir.

LA FOOLE.

  Yes, I assure you, sir.

MOROSE.

  What is true, gentlemen? What do you assure me?

DAW.

  That we have known your bride, sir—

LA FOOLE.

  In good fashion. She was our mistress, or so—   100

CLERIMONT.

  Nay, you must be plain, knights, as you were to me.

OTTER.

  Ay, the question is, if you have *carnaliter* or no.

LA FOOLE.

  Carnaliter? What else, sir?

OTTER.

  It is enough: a plain nullity.

EPICOENE.

  I am undone, I am undone!   105

MOROSE.

  Oh, let me worship and adore you, gentlemen!

EPICOENE.

  I am undone.   [*Weeps.*]

MOROSE.

  Yes, to my hand, I thank these knights: master parson, let
  me thank you otherwise.   [*Gives him money.*]

CENTAUR.

And ha' they confess'd?   110

MAVIS.

Now out upon 'em, informers!

TRUEWIT.

You see what creatures you may bestow your favors on, madams.

HAUGHTY.

I would except against 'em as beaten knights, wench, and not good witnesses in law.   115

MRS. OTTER.

Poor gentlewoman, how she takes it!

HAUGHTY.

Be comforted, Morose, I love you the better for't.

CENTAUR.

So do I, I protest.

CUTBEARD.

But, gentlemen, you have not known her since *matrimonium*?

DAW.

Not today, master doctor.   120

LA FOOLE.

No, sir, not today.

CUTBEARD.

Why then I say, for any act before, the *matrimonium* is good and perfect, unless the worshipful bridegroom did precisely before witness demand if she were *virgo ante nuptias*.

EPICOENE.

No, that he did not, I assure you, master doctor.   125

CUTBEARD.

It he cannot prove that, it is *ratum conjugium*, notwithstanding the premises. And they do no way *impedire*. And this is my sentence, this I pronounce.

OTTER.

I am of master doctor's resolution too, sir: if you made not that demand *ante nuptias*.   130

MOROSE.

Oh my heart! Wilt thou break? Wilt thou break? This is

---

126. *ratum conjugium*] valid marriage.

worst of all worst worsts that hell could have devis'd!
Marry a whore! and so much noise!

DAUPHINE.

Come, I see now plain confederacy in this doctor and this
parson to abuse a gentleman. You study his affliction. I 135
pray be gone, companions. And, gentlemen, I begin to
suspect you for having parts with 'em. Sir, will it please you
hear me?

MOROSE.

Oh, do not talk to me; take not from me the pleasure of
dying in silence, nephew.   140

DAUPHINE.

Sir, I must speak to you. I have been long your poor
despis'd kinsman, and many a hard thought has strengthen'd
you against me; but now it shall appear if either I love you
or your peace, and prefer them to all the world beside. I will
not be long or grievous to you, sir. If I free you of this 145
unhappy match absolutely and instantly after all this
trouble, and almost in your despair now—

MOROSE.

(It cannot be.)

DAUPHINE.

Sir, that you be never troubled with a murmur of it more,
what shall I hope for or deserve of you?   150

MOROSE.

Oh, what thou wilt, nephew! Thou shalt deserve me and
have me.

DAUPHINE.

Shall I have your favor perfect to me, and love hereafter?

MOROSE.

That and anything beside. Make thine own conditions. My
whole estate is thine. Manage it, I will become thy ward.   155

DAUPHINE.

Nay, sir, I will not be so unreasonable.

EPICOENE.

Will Sir Dauphine be mine enemy too?

DAUPHINE.

You know I have been long a suitor to you, uncle, that out
of your estate, which is fifteen hundred a year, you would

132. worsts] worsts! *F1.*

allow me but five hundred during life and assure the rest 160
upon me after, to which I have often by myself and friends
tender'd you a writing to sign, which you would never
consent or incline to. If you please but to effect it now—

MOROSE.

Thou shalt have it, nephew. I will do it, and more.

DAUPHINE.

If I quit you not presently and forever of this cumber, you 165
shall have power instantly, afore all these, to revoke your
act, and I will become whose slave you will give me to
forever.

MOROSE.

Where is the writing? I will seal to it, that, or to a blank,
and write thine own conditions.   170

EPICOENE.

Oh me, most unfortunate wretched gentlewoman!

HAUGHTY.

Will Sir Dauphine do this?

EPICOENE.

Good sir, have some compassion on me.

MOROSE.

Oh, my nephew knows you belike: away, crocodile

CENTAUR.

He does it not, sure, without good ground.   175

DAUPHINE.

Here sir.   [*Gives him documents.*]

MOROSE.

Come, nephew, give me the pen. I will subscribe to anything,
and seal to what thou wilt for my deliverance. Thou art my
restorer. Here, I deliver it thee as my deed. If there be a word
in it lacking or writ with false orthography, I protest before 180
God, I will not take the advantage.   [*Returns the documents.*]

165. presently] presently? *F1*.   180–181. before God,] before——
                                           F1; before heaven *Gifford*.

165. *cumber*] burden, distress.
169. *blank*] a legal document with spaces for addition of details.
180–181. *before God*] most editors, following Gifford, have taken the dash
in the text to mean "heaven," but it does not seem likely that Jonson would
have been impelled to omit such a mild expression. "God," however,
violated the statute against oaths, 1606. (See E. K. Chambers, *Elizabethan
Stage*, 1923, IV, 338–339.)

DAUPHINE.

Then here is your release, sir— (*He takes off* Epicoene's
peruke.) You have married a boy: a gentleman's son that I
have brought up this half year at my great charges, and for
this composition which I have now made with you. What 185
say you, master doctor? This is *justum impedimentum*, I hope,
error personae?

OTTER.

Yes sir, *in primo gradu.*

CUTBEARD.

In primo gradu.

DAUPHINE.

(*He pulls off their beards and disguise.*) I thank you, good 190
Doctor Cutbeard and Parson Otter. —You are beholden
to 'em, sir, that have taken this pains for you; and my friend,
Master Truewit, who enabled 'em for the business. Now
you may go in and rest, be as private as you will, sir. I'll
not trouble you till you trouble me with your funeral, which 195
I care not how soon it come.   [*Exit* Morose.]
Cutbeard, I'll make your lease good. Thank me not but with
your leg, Cutbeard. And Tom Otter, your princess shall be
reconcil'd to you. —How now, gentlemen! Do you look at
me?   200

CLERIMONT.

A boy.

DAUPHINE.

Yes, Mistress Epicoene.

TRUEWIT.

Well, Dauphine, you have lurch'd your friends of the better
half of the garland, by concealing this part of the plot! But
much good do it thee, thou deserv'st it, lad. And, Clerimont, 205
for thy unexpected bringing in these two to confession, wear
my part of it freely. Nay, Sir Daw and Sir La Foole, you
see the gentlewoman that has done you the favors! We are
all thankful to you, and so should the womankind herc,
specially for lying on her, though not with her! You meant 210

194. sir.] *followed by: Exit* Morose.
Gifford.

194–196. *I'll . . . come*] The placing of Gifford's S.D. (see textual note,
above) seems an unnecessary refinement because Dauphine is in character
when he makes these remarks directly to Morose.

so, I am sure? But that we have stuck it upon you today
in your own imagin'd persons, and so lately, this Amazon,
the champion of the sex, should beat you now thriftily for
the common slanders which ladies receive from such cuckoos
as you are. You are they that, when no merit or fortune can 215
make you hope to enjoy their bodies, will yet lie with their
reputations and make their fame suffer. Away, you common
moths of these and all ladies' honors. Go, travail to make
legs and faces, and come home with some new matter to be
laugh'd at: you deserve to live in an air as corrupted as 220
that wherewith you feed rumor. [*Exeunt* Daw *and* La
Foole.] Madams, you are mute upon this new metamorphosis! but here stands she that has vindicated your
fames. Take heed of such *insectae* hereafter. And let it not
trouble you that you have discover'd any mysteries to this 225
young gentleman. He is (a'most) of years, and will make a
good visitant within this twelvemonth. In the meantime
we'll all undertake for his secrecy, that can speak so well
of his silence. [*Coming forward.*] Spectators, if you like this
comedy, rise cheerfully, and now Morose is gone in, clap 230
your hands. It may be that noise will cure him, at least
please him.   [*Exeunt.*]

THE END

This Comedy was first
acted in the year   235
1609.

By the Children of her Majesty's
Revels.

The principal Comedians were,

Nat. Field ⎫	⎧ Will. Barksted	240
Gil. Carie ⎪	⎪ Will. Pen.	
Hug. Attawel ⎬	⎨ Ric. Allin	
Joh. Smith ⎭	⎩ Joh. Blaney	

With the allowance of the Master of Revels.

218. travail] travel *F3*.

---

218. *travail*] the original spelling (travaile) of *travel* exposes the root
meaning.

Appendix A

Historical Collation of Editions

The following notes list the substantive variations of F1(o) (origina setting of F1 1616), F1(r) (resettings of certain sheets of F1 1616), Q (1620), F2 (1640), F3 (1692), and MS1 (for "Still to be neat" Folger manuscript V.a.162), MS2 (for "Still to be neat" New York Public Library manuscript Drexel 4041) from the text of this edition. Since Herford and Simpson's edition (volume V, 1937) is the standard modern text, I list their substantive errors here too, siglum H.S.; most of their errors can be traced to the edition by Miss A. Henry (1906), which must have served as printer's copy for the last three acts. Semi-substantive variations are excluded, and spellings are modernized, except in a few cases where the old spelling helps to show the relationship between variants. Omission of a siglum after the bracket indicates that the reading of the edition in question agrees with the text.

[Dedication]
4. by cause] because *F3*.

[Prologue]
8. make ... feasts] (make ... feasts) *F1(r)*, *Q*.
9. tastes] taste *F2–3*.

[Another Prologue]
0.1] *Occasion'd . . . exception*]   *om.*
F1(o), *F2–3*.

[Persons of the Play]
1. no] *om. F1(r)*; not *F2–3*.
12. *Collegiates*]   Collegiate   *F1(r)*,
F2–3.
13. MISTRESS] MAD. *F2–3*.
14. MISTRESS TRUSTY] MRS. MAVIS
F1(r), *F2–3*.

[I.i]
5. pray] pay *Q*.
13. in to] into *Q*, *F2–3*.
29. article] particle *F2–3*.

34.] Horses o' the time *marginal note not in F1(o)*, *F2–3*.
35. spend] speak *F2–3*.
45. our] ou *Q*.
57. nor hear] not hear *F1(o)*, *F2–3*.
64. Well, sir,] Well, sir. *F1–3*, *Q*.
69. but] bt *Q*.
82. scour'd] sour'd *F1(o)*.
89. causes] secrets *MS1*.
90. sweet] well *MS1*.
91. look] form *MS1*.
93. flowing] hanging *MS1*.
94. Such] Those *MS1*.
94. neglect] neglects *MS1–2*.
94. taketh] please *MS1*.
95. all th'] those *MS1*.
96. They] Thy *F1(r)*.
96.] Those eyes delight, but these the heart *MS1*.
113. serves] serve *Q*.
150. upon] up on *F1(r)*, *Q*; on *F1(o)*, *F2–3*.
151. quit] quiet *F3*.

158. sir,] sir! *F1(r)*, *Q*; sir? *F1(o)*, *F2–3*.
161. in] *om. F1(o)*, *F2–3*.
168. marching] going *F1(o)*, *F2–3*.

[I.ii]
12. thee] the *F3*.
32. one Cutbeard] *om. F1(o)*, *F2–3*.
37. continence] continency *F2–3*.
38. eminent] emient *Q*.
58. do] *om. F2–3*.

[I.iii]
36. presents] persents *F1(o)*.
39. for there] their *F1(o)*, *F2–3*.
43. Sir] Sis *F1(o)*.
44. below] *om. F1(o)*, *F2–3*.
44. owns] owes *F1(o)*, *F2*.

[I.iv]
15. but] *om. F1(o)*, *F2–3*.
35. of the west] o' the west *Q*.
38. for] *om. F1(o)*, *F2–3*.
66. S.P. LA FOOLE] CLE. *F1(o)*, *F2–3*.
72. wind-fucker] wind-sucker *F3*.
73. mistress] master *F2–3*.

[II.i]
13. your answer] you answer *F2–3*.
22. your] you *F1(o)*.
37.1–39. S.D.] One winds a horn without. Again. *Marginal note F1–2*; One winds a horn without again. *F3, at l. 39*.
45. with] *om. F1(o)*, *F2–3*.

[II.ii]
32. preachings] parleys *F1(o)*, *F2–3*.
36. frosty] frostie *Q*.
61. to] too *F1–2*.
61. young, and] and young, *Q*.
87. your] you *F3*.
115. demonstration:] demonstration *F1–3*, *Q*.
130. rinses] rises *F1–3*, *Q*.

[II.iii]
21. works] work *Q*.

53. There's] There is *F1 (uncorr.)*.
107. and] are *F2–3*.
109. S.P. DAW.] DAV. *F1, Dauph. Q*.
124. procreation] proceation *F1*.
126. you'll] you you'll *F1, Q*.

[II.iv]
45. to humanity] or humanity *F2–3*.
47. S.P. CLERIMONT.] DLE. *F1*.
48. S.P. DAUPHINE.] CAUP. *F1*.
60. your] our *F2–3*.
87. miracle] a miracle *F2–3*.
116. She ... him, sir] Sir, she ... him *F2–3*.
137. Hang him] *om. Q*.

[II.v]
1. your] you *F1*.
23. happly] happely *F1*; happily *Q*.
26. ears] ear *Q*.
68. heicfar] heifar *F2–3*.

[II.vi]
19. now;] now *F1, Q*.

[III.i]
15. 'em] them *Q*.
21. horse this.] horse. *Q*; horse, this *F2–3*.

[III.ii]
40. pith] pitch *F2–3*.
51. judg'd] adjudg'd *Q*.

[III.iii]
1. Why,] Why *F1–2*.
1. not] *om. F2–3*.
17. S.P. DAW.] DAVP. *F1, Q*; DAU. *F2–3*.
24. should] would *F2–3*.
31. main] man *F1–3*, *Q*.
56. S.P. DAUPHINE] DAV. *F1*; DAW. *Q*.
65. it] *om. Q*.
82. we] he *F2–3*.

[III.iv]
12. God] Good *H.S.*

[III.v]
17. you] your *F3*.
43. reverend] reveverend *F1*.

48. feast] feasting *F2–3.*
110. yet hang] be hang'd *F3.*

[III.vi]
85. promis'd] promise *F3.*
105. to] too *F1–3, Q.*

[III.vii]
2.1.] *Music of sorts. F3.*
16.1.] *marginal note at l. 16 F1(r);
at l. 20 F2–3.*
24. guests] guess *F3.*

[IV.i]
4. a] *om. F3.*
63. diffidence] difference *F2–3.*
82. she then] then she *F2–3.*
84. all ways] alwaies *F1–3, Q.*

[IV.ii]
13. Now] Pray *H.S.*
20. Oh,] O, *F1;* O' *Q.*
23. again] against *F2–3.*
50. S.P. DAUPHINE.] DAW. *Q.*
93. S.D. *beats] beats upon Q.*

[IV.iv]
2. S.P. DAUPHINE.] DAV. *F1;*
DAW. *Q.*
12. i' the Cockpit] in a Cock-pit
F1 (uncorr.).
20. so] *om. Q.*
36. and't] and *F3.*
72. him] her *Q.*
154. posts] post *F2–3.*
167. S.P. TRUEWIT.] CLE. *Q.*

[IV.v]
12. lords] the lords *F2–3.*
21. scratch] search *F2–3.*
30. the arras] he arras *F3.*
84. Jack Daw!] Jack! *F2–3.*
90. But] And *H.S.*
115.1. *come] came F1–3, Q.*
120. S.P. DAUPHINE.] DAW. *Q.*
123. loss] less *F2.*
124. good] goods *Q.*
272. you, you] you *F1–2, Q.*

284. places] place *F2.*

[IV.vi]
24. brake] barke *F2–3.*
42. engine] engineer *Q.*
45. There's] There is *F2–3.*
98. S.P. MRS. OTTER.] Mrs. OT.
F1; Mrs. T. *H.S.*

[IV.vii]
16. intergatories] interrogatories
F2–3.
18. calm] *om. Q.*
23. S.P. TRUEWIT.] *om. Q.*
24. in] *om. F3.*
33. sir—] sir: *F1–3, Q.*

[V.i]
16. squire] square *F3.*

[V.ii]
3. so] *om. Q.*
8. Are … stones?] (Are … stones?)
F1–3, Q.
58. continue] continue you *Q.*

[V.iii]
7. once] once again *Q.*
55. impertinencies] pertinencies
F1 (uncorr.); impertinences *Q.*
60. motion] about motion *Q.*
68. *divertendo] divertendendo F2–3.*
180. *frigiditate] frigitate F3.*

[V.iv]
25. list] lists *F2–3.*
83. -like] -like-like *Q.*
132. worsts] worsts! *F1–3, Q.*
161. friends] my friends *F2–3.*
165. presently] presently? *F1, Q;*
presently, *F2–3.*
180–181. before God] before——
F1–3, Q.
206. in] *om. F2–3.*
215. or] of *F2–3.*
218. travail] travel *F3.*
234–244. *om. Q, F2–3; the list of
actors follows the dramatis personae in
F2–3.*

Appendix B

Chronology

Approximate years are indicated by *, occurrences in doubt by (?).

Political and Literary Events	Life and Works of Ben Jonson
1558 Accession of Queen Elizabeth I. Thomas Kyd born. Robert Greene born.	
1560 George Chapman born.	
1561 Francis Bacon born.	
1564 Shakespeare born. Christopher Marlowe born.	
1570 Thomas Heywood born.*	
1572 Thomas Dekker born.* John Donne born. Massacre of St. Bartholomew's Day.	
1573	Benjamin Jonson born in London, about June 11, posthumous son of a clergyman. His mother remarried a bricklayer.
1576 The Theatre, the first permanent public theater in London, established by James Burbage. John Marston born.	
1577 The Curtain theater opened. Holinshed's *Chronicles of England, Scotland and Ireland*.	

Drake begins circumnavigation of
the earth; completed 1580.

1579
John Fletcher born.
John Lyly's *Euphues: The Anatomy of Wit.*

1580
Thomas Middleton born.

1583
Philip Massinger born.

1584
Francis Beaumont born.*

1586
Death of Sir Philip Sidney.
John Ford born.

1587
The Rose theater opened by Henslowe.
Marlowe's *TAMBURLAINE*, Part I.*
Greene's *ALPHONSUS KING OF ARAGON.*
Execution of Mary, Queen of Scots.

Attends Westminster School, studying under William Camden, one of the most learned men in England.*

1588
Defeat of the Spanish Armada.
Marlowe's *TAMBURLAINE*, Part II.*

Leaves Westminster School; apprenticed as bricklayer.*

1589
Marlowe's *THE JEW OF MALTA.*
Greene's *FRIAR BACON AND FRIAR BUNGAY.*
Kyd's *THE SPANISH TRAGEDY.*

1590
Spenser's *Faerie Queene* (Books I–III) published.
Sidney's *Arcadia* published.
Shakespeare's *HENRY VI*, Parts I–III,* *TITUS ANDRONICUS.*
Greene's *GEORGE-A-GREENE*(?).*

1591
Shakespeare's *RICHARD III.*
Greene's *ORLANDO FURIOSO,* *JAMES THE FOURTH.*

1591–1592

Serves as a soldier in the Low Countries.*

1592
Marlowe's *DOCTOR FAUSTUS**
and *EDWARD II.**
Shakespeare's *TAMING OF THE
SHREW** and *THE COMEDY OF
ERRORS.**
Death of Robert Greene.

1593
Shakespeare's *LOVE'S LABOR'S
LOST;** *Venus and Adonis* published.
Death of Marlowe.
Theaters closed on account of
plague.

1594
Shakespeare's *TWO GENTLE-
MEN OF VERONA;** *The Rape of
Lucrece* published.
Shakespeare's company becomes
Lord Chamberlain's Men.
James Shirley born.*
Death of Kyd.

Marries Anne Lewis.

1595
The Swan theater built.
Sidney's *Defense of Poesy* published.
Shakespeare's *ROMEO AND
JULIET,** *A MIDSUMMER
NIGHT'S DREAM,** *RICHARD
II.**
Raleigh's first expedition to Guiana.

Serves as an actor in one of the
London companies.*

1596
Spenser's *Faerie Queene* (Books IV–
VI) published.
Shakespeare's *MERCHANT OF
VENICE,** *KING JOHN.**

Collaborated on plays, some for the
Admiral's Men.*

1597
Bacon's *Essays* (first edition).
Shakespeare's *HENRY IV*, Part I.*

Imprisoned for part authorship of
a lost play, *THE ISLE OF DOGS.*

1598
Demolition of the Theatre.
Shakespeare's *MUCH ADO
ABOUT NOTHING;** *HENRY
IV*, Part II.*
Seven books of Chapman's trans-
lation of the *Iliad* published.

THE CASE IS ALTERED (Children
of Chapel Royal).*
EVERY MAN IN HIS HUMOR
(Lord Chamberlain's Men).
Kills Gabriel Spencer, a fellow
actor, in a duel; imprisoned but

freed on plea of benefit of clergy; converted to Roman Catholicism while in jail.

1599

The Globe theater opened.
Shakespeare's *AS YOU LIKE IT,* *HENRY V,* *JULIUS CAESAR.* *
Dekker's *THE SHOEMAKERS' HOLIDAY.* *
Death of Spenser.

EVERY MAN OUT OF HIS HUMOR (Lord Chamberlain's Men) starts a vogue in satiric comedy.

1600

Shakespeare's *TWELFTH NIGHT,* *HAMLET.* *
Marston's *ANTONIO AND MEL-LIDA,* *ANTONIO'S REVENGE.* *
The Fortune theater built by Alleyn.

CYNTHIA'S REVELS (Children of Chapel Royal).

1601

Shakespeare's *MERRY WIVES OF WINDSOR.* *
Insurrection and execution of the Earl of Essex.

POETASTER (Children of Chapel Royal).
Publicly feuds with Marston and Dekker in the War of the Theaters.

1602

Shakespeare's *TROILUS AND CRESIDA,* *ALL'S WELL THAT ENDS WELL.* *

1603

Death of Queen Elizabeth I; accession of James VI of Scotland as James I.
Florio's translation of Montaigne's *Essays* published.
Heywood's *A WOMAN KILLED WITH KINDNESS.*
Marston's *THE MALCONTENT.* *
Shakespeare's company becomes the King's Men.

SEJANUS (King's Men) hissed off the stage.
Son Benjamin dies, aged six.
Forms "The Mermaid Club" and gathers a coterie about him.

1604

Shakespeare's *MEASURE FOR MEASURE,* *OTHELLO.* *
Marston's *THE FAWN.* *
Chapman's *BUSSY D'AMBOIS.* *

1605

Shakespeare's *KING LEAR.* *
Marston's *THE DUTCH COUR-TESAN.* *
Bacon's *Advancement of Learning* published.

Early masque at court, *THE MASQUE OF BLACKNESS.*
EASTWARD HO, in collaboration with Chapman and Marston (Children of the Queen's Revels); Jonson

APPENDIX B

The Gunpowder Plot.

and Chapman imprisoned because of alleged derogatory allusions to King James.

1606
Shakespeare's *MACBETH.**
Tourneur's *REVENGER'S TRAG-EDY.**
The Red Bull theater built.

VOLPONE (King's Men).*

1607
Shakespeare's *ANTONY AND CLEOPATRA.**
Beaumont's *KNIGHT OF THE BURNING PESTLE.**
Settlement of Jamestown, Virginia.

VOLPONE performed at Oxford and Cambridge.*

1608
Shakespeare's *CORIOLANUS,** *TIMON OF ATHENS,** *PERICLES.**
Chapman's *CONSPIRACY AND TRAGEDY OF CHARLES, DUKE OF BYRON.**
Richard Burbage leases Blackfriars Theatre for King Company.
John Milton born.

1609
Shakespeare's *CYMBELINE;** *Sonnets* published.

EPICOENE (Children of the Queen's Revels).

1610
Chapman's *REVENGE OF BUSSY D'AMBOIS.**

THE ALCHEMIST (King's Men).
Returns to Anglican religion.*

1611
Authorized (King James) Version of the Bible published.
Shakespeare's *THE WINTER'S TALE,** *THE TEMPEST.**
Beaumont and Fletcher's *A KING AND NO KING.*
Tourneur's *ATHEIST'S TRAG-EDY.**

CATILINE (King's Men) damned by theater audiences, but later greatly respected by readers.
Writing masques for Court entertainments regularly up to 1625.

1612
Webster's *THE WHITE DEVIL.**

1612–1613

Travels in France as tutor to son of Sir Walter Raleigh.

1613
The Globe theater burned.

Shakespeare's *HENRY VIII* (with Fletcher).
Webster's *THE DUCHESS OF MALFI.**
Middleton's *A CHASTE MAID IN CHEAPSIDE.*

1614
The Globe theater rebuilt.
The Hope theater built.

BARTHOLOMEW FAIR (Lady Elizabeth's Men).

1616
Death of Shakespeare.
Death of Beaumont.

THE DEVIL IS AN ASS (King's Men).
Publication of Folio edition of *Works* ridiculed for its pretension.
Receives royal pension, and henceforth he is considered poet laureate, although he never styled himself such.

1618
Outbreak of Thirty Years War.
Execution of Raleigh.
1618–1619

Journeys on foot to Scotland; visits there with William Drummond.

1619

Given honorary M.A. by Oxford University.

1620
Pilgrim Fathers land at Plymouth.

1621
Middleton's *WOMEN BEWARE WOMEN.**

1622
Middleton and Rowley's *THE CHANGELING.**

1623
Publication of Folio edition of Shakespeare's *COMEDIES, HISTORIES, AND TRAGEDIES.*

Lectures on rhetoric at Gresham College in London(?).
Books and manuscripts lost when lodgings burn.

1625
Death of King James I; accession of Charles I.
Death of Fletcher.

1626
Death of Tourneur.

THE STAPLE OF NEWS (King's Men).

1627
Death of Middleton.

1628
Ford's *THE LOVER'S MELAN-CHOLY.*

Paralyzed by a stroke.
Appointed chronologer of the City of London.

1629

THE NEW INN (King's Men).

1631
Shirley's *THE TRAITOR.*
Death of Donne.

Quarrels with Inigo Jones.

1632
Death of Dekker.*

THE MAGNETIC LADY (King's Men).

1633
Donne's *Poems* published.
Massinger's *THE CITY MADAM.**

A TALE OF A TUB, revised from an earlier play (Queen Henrietta's Men).

1634
Death of Chapman, Marston, Webster.*

A final "entertainment," *LOVE'S WELCOME AT BOLSOVER.*

1637

Jonson dies in Westminster, August 6; buried in Westminster Abbey, August 9.

1638

Jonsonus Virbius, a memorial volume, published.

1640
Death of Massinger.
1640–1641

Works published, two volumes, folio, by Sir Kenelm Digby.

1641
Death of Heywood.

1642
Shirley's *THE COURT SECRET.*
All theaters closed by Act of Parliament.